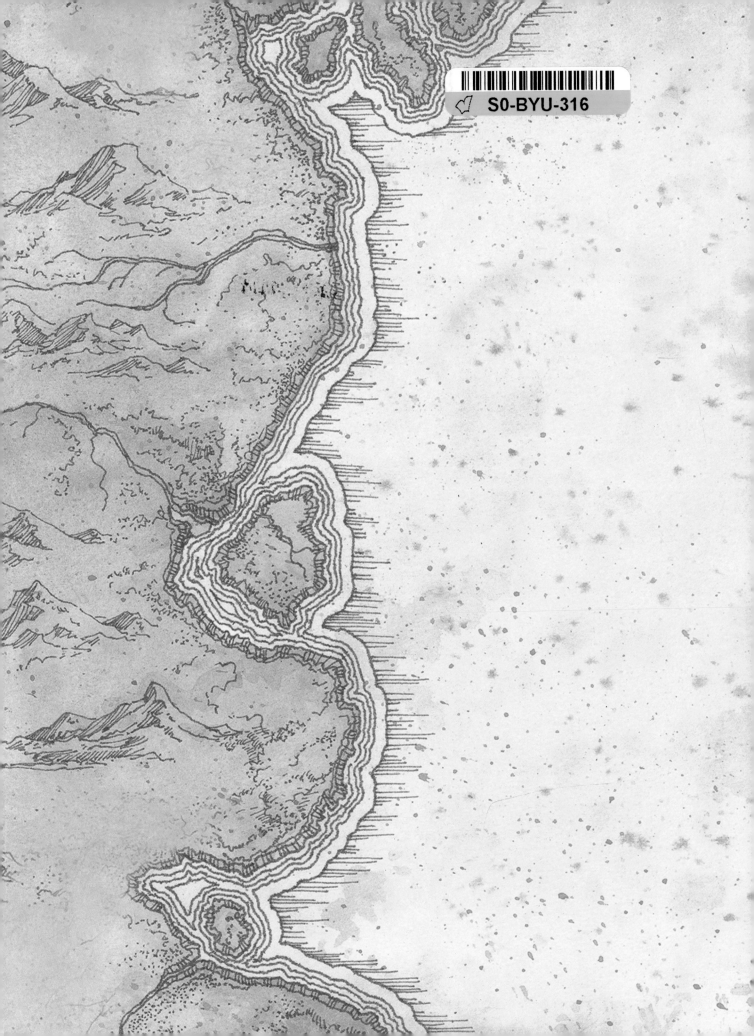

Meeting Many People

Series Authors
Dr. Richard G. Boehm
Claudia Hoone
Dr. Thomas M. McGowan
Dr. Mabel C. McKinney-Browning
Dr. Ofelia B. Miramontes

Consultants for Primary Grades
Carol Hamilton Cobb
Janet J. Eubank
Billie M. Kapp

Series Consultants
Dr. Alma Flor Ada
Dr. Phillip Bacon
Dr. W. Dorsey Hammond
Dr. Asa Grant Hilliard, III

HARCOURT BRACE & COMPANY
Orlando Atlanta Austin Boston San Francisco Chicago Dallas
New York Toronto London

SERIES AUTHORS

Dr. Richard G. Boehm
Professor
Department of Geography and
Planning
Southwest Texas State University
San Marcos, Texas

Claudia Hoone
Teacher
Ralph Waldo Emerson School #58
Indianapolis, Indiana

Dr. Thomas M. McGowan
Associate Professor
Division of Curriculum and Instruction
Arizona State University
Tempe, Arizona

Dr. Mabel C. McKinney-Browning
Director
Division of Public Education
American Bar Association
Chicago, Illinois

Dr. Ofelia B. Miramontes
Associate Professor
School of Education
University of Colorado
Boulder, Colorado

SERIES CONSULTANTS

Dr. Alma Flor Ada
Professor
School of Education
University of San Francisco
San Francisco, California

Dr. Phillip Bacon
Professor Emeritus of Geography
and Anthropology
University of Houston
Houston, Texas

Dr. W. Dorsey Hammond
Professor of Education
Oakland University
Rochester, Michigan

Dr. Asa Grant Hilliard, III
Fuller E. Callaway Professor of
Urban Education
Georgia State University
Atlanta, Georgia

MEDIA AND LITERATURE SPECIALISTS

Dr. Joseph A. Braun, Jr.
Professor of Elementary Social Studies
Department of Curriculum and
Instruction
Illinois State University
Normal, Illinois

Meridith McGowan
Youth Librarian
Tempe Public Library
Tempe, Arizona

GRADE-LEVEL CONSULTANTS AND REVIEWERS

Esther Booth-Cross
School-Wide Coordinator
Bond Elementary School
Chicago, Illinois

Carol Hamilton Cobb
Teacher
Gateway School
Metropolitan Nashville Public Schools
Madison, Tennessee

Nodjie Conner
Teacher
Old Richmond Elementary School
Tobaccoville, North Carolina

Janet J. Eubank
Language Arts Curriculum Specialist
Wichita Public Schools
Wichita, Kansas

Mary Fran Goetz
Teacher
Notre Dame de Sion
Kansas City, Missouri

Billie M. Kapp
Teacher
Coventry Grammar School
Coventry, Connecticut

Mickey McConnell
Teacher
Central Heights Elementary School
Blountsville, Tennessee

Gwen Mitsui
Teacher
Solomon Elementary School
Wahiawa, Hawaii

Wanda Joyce Owen
Teacher
Sallie Curtis Elementary School
Beaumont, Texas

Ronald R. Paul
Curriculum Director, Retired
Mehlville School District
St. Louis, Missouri

J. Mark Stewart
Social Studies Supervisor
Columbus Public Schools
Columbus, Ohio

Angie G. Trevino
Assistant Principal
Longoria Elementary School
Pharr, Texas

Kathy Tubb
Teacher
South Elementary School
Levelland, Texas

Requests for permission to make copies of any part of the work should be mailed to: Permissions Department, Harcourt Brace & Company, 6277 Sea Harbor Drive, Orlando, Florida 32887-6777.

HARCOURT BRACE and Quill Design is a registered trademark of Harcourt Brace & Company.

Acknowledgments and other credits appear in the back of this book.

Printed in the United States of America

ISBN: 0-15-302038-5

3 4 5 6 7 8 9 10   032   99 98 97

CONTENTS

F.Y.I.

Literature and Primary Sources

Skills

Features

Maps

Charts, Graphs, Diagrams, Tables, and Time Lines

ATLAS

Geo Georgie wants to invite you to visit new places this year. The maps in this book will help you to know where you are. When you see Geo Georgie, stop and learn how to use the maps.

Come back to this Atlas as you journey through Stories in Time.

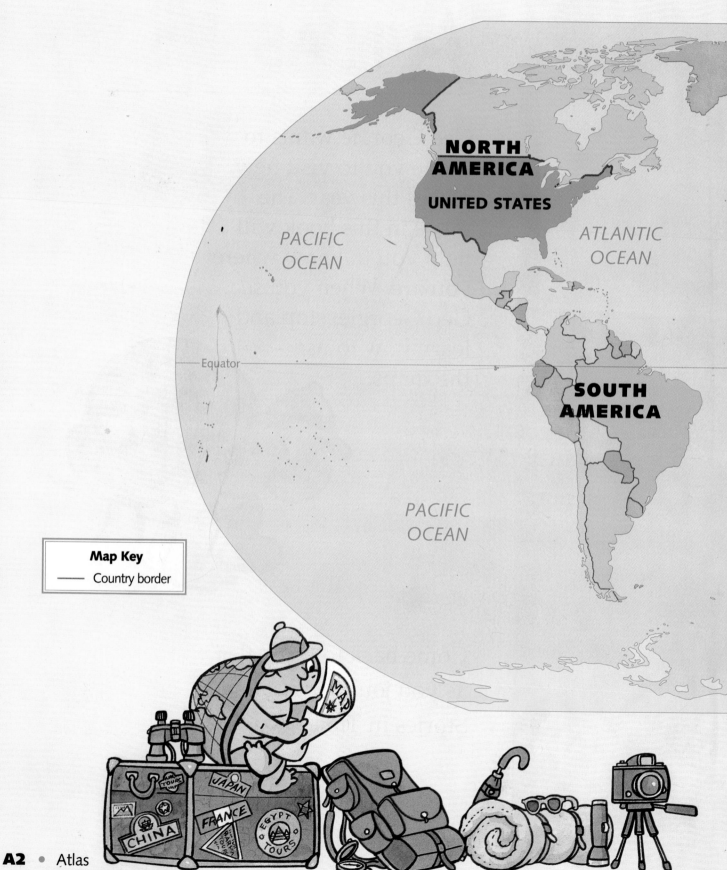

NORTH
AMERICA

UNITED STATES

PACIFIC
OCEAN

ATLANTIC
OCEAN

Equator

SOUTH
AMERICA

PACIFIC
OCEAN

Map Key
—— Country border

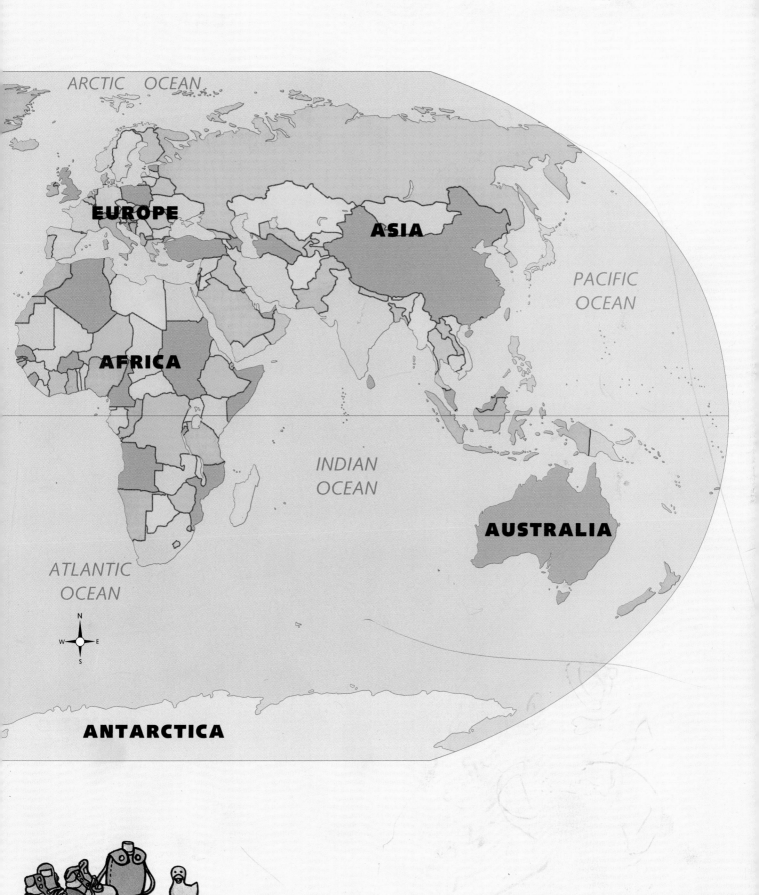

ARCTIC OCEAN

EUROPE

ASIA

PACIFIC OCEAN

AFRICA

INDIAN OCEAN

AUSTRALIA

ATLANTIC OCEAN

N
W—E
S

ANTARCTICA

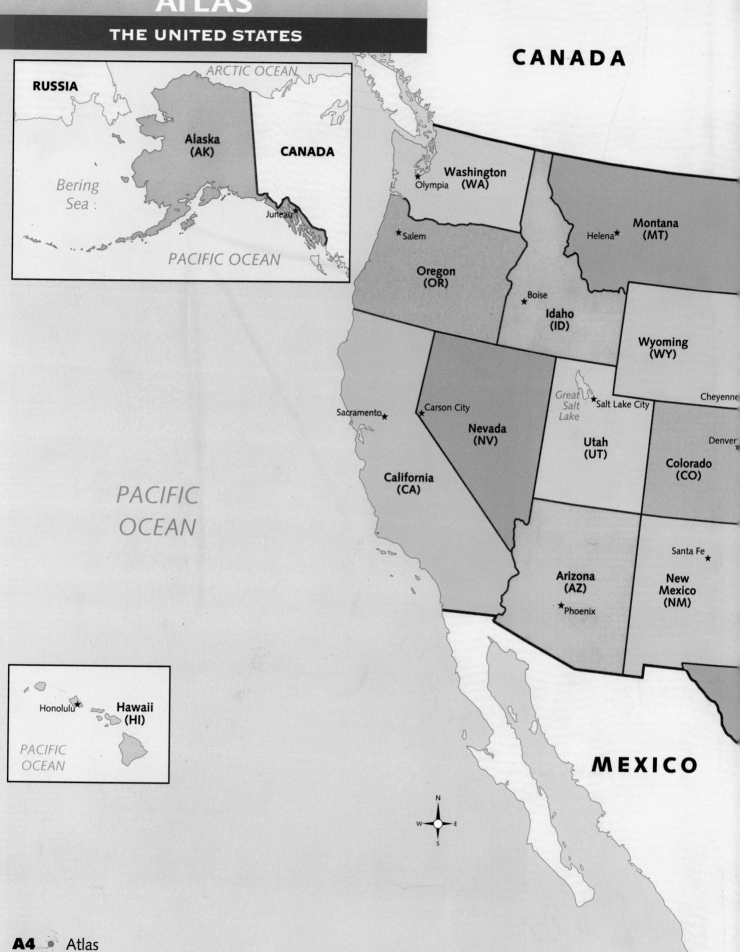

RUSSIA

ARCTIC OCEAN

Alaska
(AK)

CANADA

Bering
Sea

Juneau★

PACIFIC OCEAN

PACIFIC
OCEAN

Honolulu★ Hawaii
(HI)

PACIFIC
OCEAN

CANADA

Washington
(WA)
Olympia★

Montana
(MT)
Helena★

★Salem

Oregon
(OR)

Boise★

Idaho
(ID)

Wyoming
(WY)

Great
Salt
Lake ★Salt Lake City

Cheyenne

Sacramento★

Carson City
★

Nevada
(NV)

Utah
(UT)

Denver

Colorado
(CO)

California
(CA)

Santa Fe
★

Arizona
(AZ)
★Phoenix

New
Mexico
(NM)

MEXICO

N
W ★ E
S

CANADA

North Dakota (ND)
★ Bismarck

Minnesota (MN)
St. Paul ★

Lake Superior

Michigan

Lake Michigan

Lake Huron

Wisconsin (WI)
Madison ★

(MI)
Lansing ★

Lake Ontario

Lake Erie

Maine (ME)
Augusta ★

Vermont (VT)
Montpelier ★

New Hampshire (NH)
★ Concord

New York (NY)
Albany ★

Boston ★

Massachusetts (MA)
★ Providence

Rhode Island (RI)

Hartford ★
Connecticut (CT)

South Dakota (SD)
★ Pierre

Iowa (IA)
Des Moines ★

Illinois (IL)
Springfield ★

Indiana (IN)
Indianapolis ★

Ohio (OH)
Columbus ★

Pennsylvania (PA)
Harrisburg ★

Trenton ★

New Jersey (NJ)

Nebraska (NE)
Lincoln ★

West Virginia (WV)
Charleston ★

Annapolis ★
Washington, D.C. ✪
Maryland (MD)

Dover ★

Delaware (DE)

Kansas (KS)
Topeka ★

Missouri (MO)
Jefferson City ★

Kentucky (KY)
Frankfort ★

Richmond ★
Virginia (VA)

Nashville ★

Raleigh ★

North Carolina (NC)

Oklahoma (OK)
Oklahoma City ★

Arkansas (AR)
Little Rock ★

Tennessee (TN)

Columbia ★

South Carolina (SC)

Atlanta ★

Texas (TX)
Austin ★

Mississippi (MS)
Jackson ★

Alabama (AL)
Montgomery ★

Georgia (GA)

ATLANTIC OCEAN

Louisiana (LA)
Baton Rouge ★

Tallahassee ★

Florida (FL)

BAHAMAS

Gulf of Mexico

CUBA

PACIFIC OCEAN

ATLANTIC OCEAN

Greenland (DENMARK)

Alaska (UNITED STATES)

CANADA

UNITED STATES

Hawaii (UNITED STATES)

MEXICO

BAHAMAS

CUBA

DOMINICAN REPUBLIC

Puerto Rico (UNITED STATES)

JAMAICA

BELIZE

HONDURAS

HAITI

GUATEMALA

EL SALVADOR

NICARAGUA

COSTA RICA

PANAMA

TRINIDAD AND TOBAGO

VENEZUELA

GUYANA

SURINAME

FRENCH GUIANA (FRANCE)

COLOMBIA

Equator

Galápagos Islands (ECUADOR)

ECUADOR

PERU

BRAZIL

BOLIVIA

PACIFIC OCEAN

PARAGUAY

CHILE

URUGUAY

ARGENTINA

ATLANTIC OCEAN

Falkland Islands (UNITED KINGDOM)

South Georgia (UNITED KINGDOM)

N
W E
S

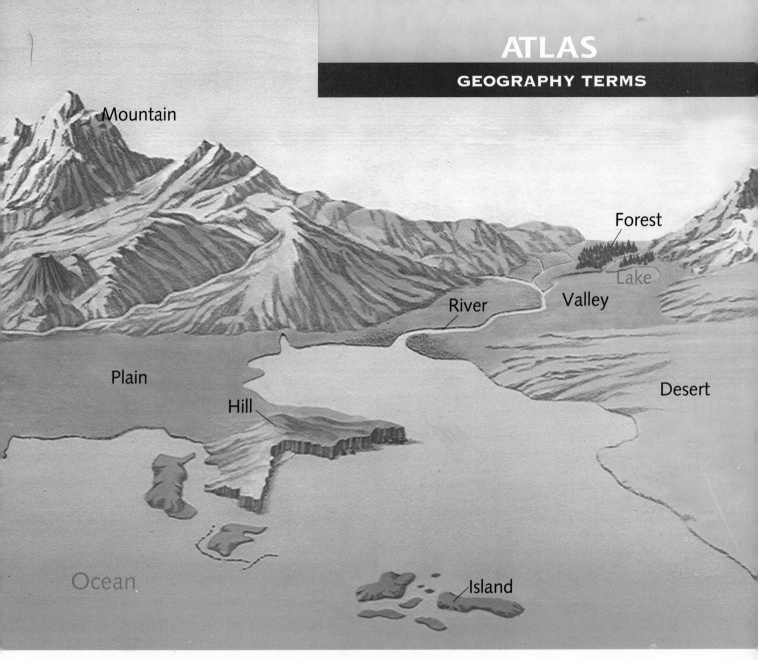

Mountain

Forest

Lake

Valley

River

Plain

Hill

Desert

Ocean

Island

desert dry land with few plants

forest large area of land where many trees grow

hill land that rises above the land around it

island land that has water on all sides

lake body of water with land on all sides

mountain highest kind of land

ocean body of salt water that covers a large area

plain flat land

river large stream of water that flows across the land

valley low land between hills or mountains

We Belong to Many Groups

VOCABULARY

group

law

STOP

community

map

goods

services

1

SET the SCENE
with Literature

Sing a Song of People

by Lois Lenski

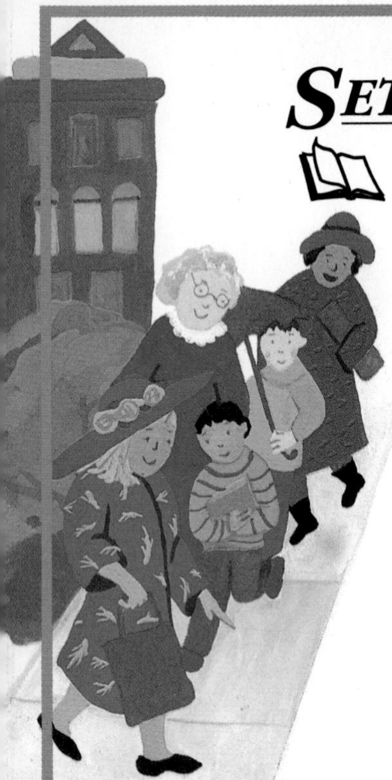

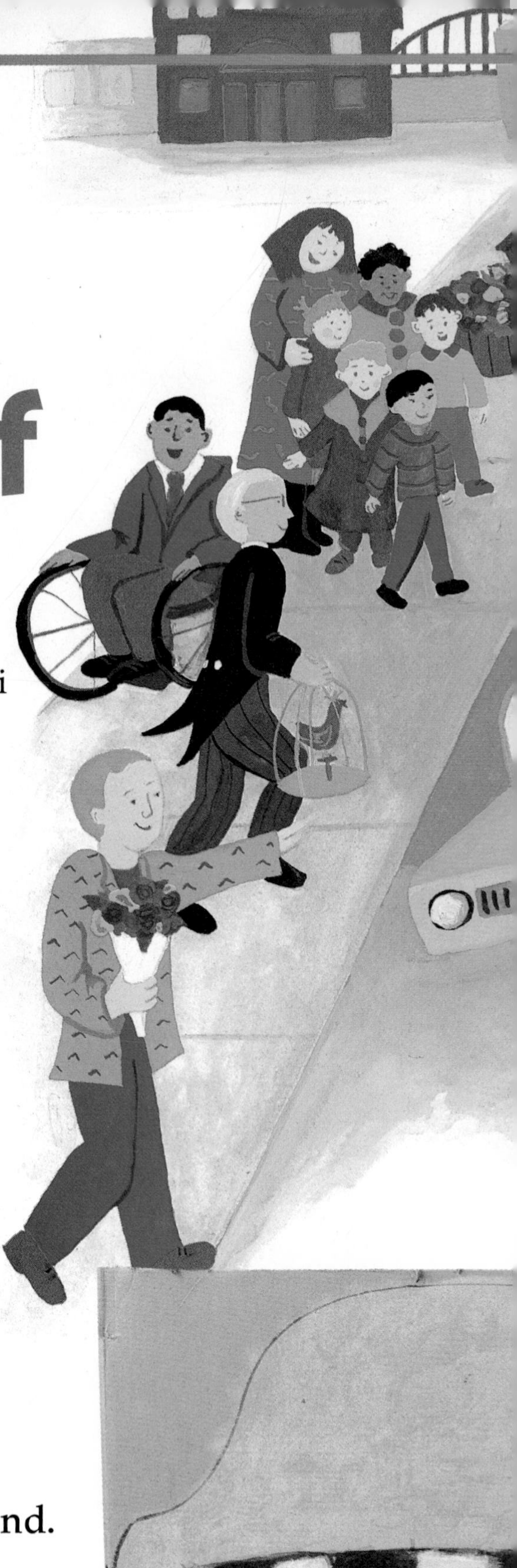

Sing a song of people
Walking fast or slow;
People in the city,
Up and down they go.

People on the sidewalk,
People on the bus;
People passing, passing,
In back and front of us.
People on the subway
Underneath the ground;
People riding taxis
Round and round and round.

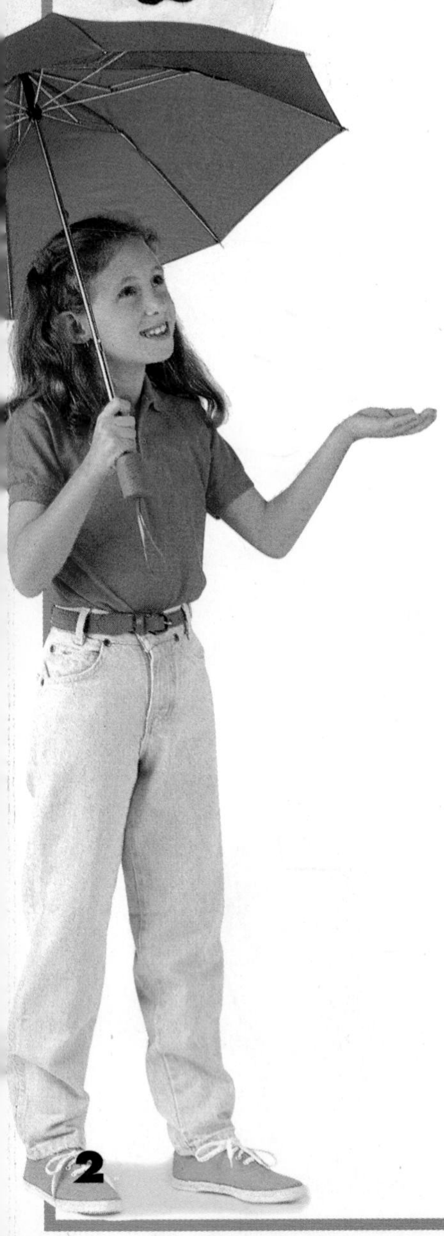

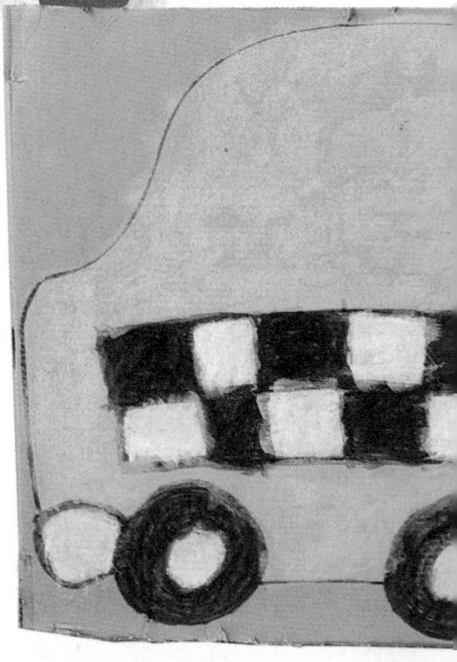

People with their hats on,
Going in the doors;
People with umbrellas
When it rains and pours.
People in tall buildings
And in stores below;
Riding elevators
Up and down they go.

People walking singly,
People in a crowd;
People saying nothing,
People talking loud.
People laughing, smiling,
Grumpy people too;
People who just hurry
And never look at you!

Sing a song of people
Who like to come and go;
Sing of city people
You see but never know!

Learning Together at School ← 1. title

2. story →

Visitors are coming to our classroom. We want to show what we can do. First, our teacher, Mrs. Warren, helps us make a plan. For some jobs we will work alone. For other jobs we will work together in a group.

3. picture

4. new word

We all make name tags for our desks. We get help from our art teacher.

Judy works on a calendar to show the activities of our busy class. She has marked our Open House on September 30.

My group is making a mural to hang on the wall. We want to show what we learn in school.

5. main idea →

6. detail →

Everyone in my group has a special job to do. Juan is the leader. A **leader** makes sure the group follows the rules. **Rules** help us listen, share, and work together fairly.

Sandy and I make a list of the scenes we want to show on our mural. Then the rest of our group helps draw and paint the mural. Finally, we all clean the room and enjoy our work.

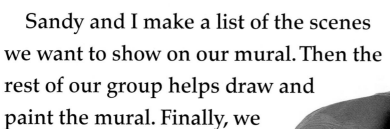

How do you learn together in your classroom?

Living at Home and in the Neighborhood

You are part of other groups, such as your family and your neighborhood. A **neighborhood** is a place where people live. Lisa is making a model of her neighborhood. Read what she says about her home and neighbors.

8

My family works together to meet our **needs**. We need food and clothing and a safe place to live. Grandma works at the neighborhood market. Dad builds buildings. They earn money to pay for the things we need.

We all work to make our home a nice place to live. My sister and I help. Linsey helps cook the meals and make the beds. I walk the dog and take out the trash. We take turns watering the plants.

People in a neighborhood help each other, too. Our neighbor Ms. Lee gives me piano lessons. I feed her cat when she visits her daughter.

Our next-door neighbor is a firefighter. He helps save lives and homes in our neighborhood. Other people work as police officers to help keep our neighborhood safe.

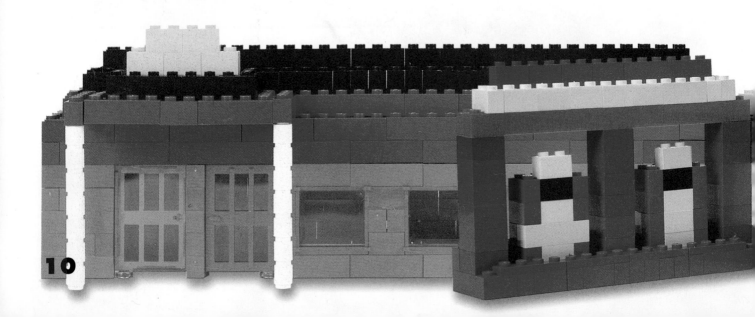

Many places in the neighborhood help us meet our needs. We have a food store and a gas station. Sometimes we eat at the restaurant.

My neighborhood is part of a community. A **community** is a place where people live, work, play, and help each other.

How is your neighborhood like Lisa's neighborhood?

SKILLS

HOW TO

Learn from a Picture and a Map

We can learn about a neighborhood by looking at a photograph.

1. Look at this photo. Tell what you see.

2. Think about how the photo was taken. Do you think you can see more from the air or the ground?

3. A **map** is a drawing that shows how a place looks from above. How are the photo and the map the same?

4. What things do you see in the photo that are not on the map?

Make a list of the places you see in the photo and on the map.

In and Around the City

LESSON

Today Jesse went into the city with his mom. A **city** is a very large community with many neighborhoods. Read Jesse's journal to find out what he discovered.

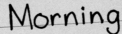

Morning

Time to go into the city. I fastened my safety belt.

Many cars, trucks, and buses are on the expressway. I wonder where they are all going.

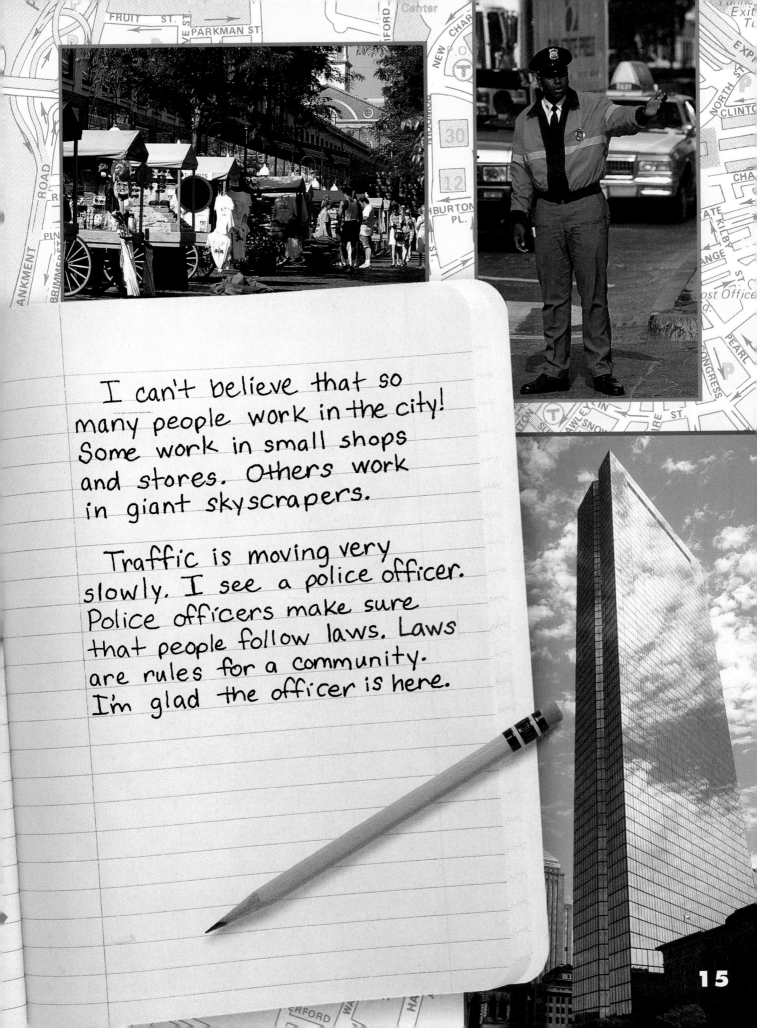

I can't believe that so many people work in the city! Some work in small shops and stores. Others work in giant skyscrapers.

Traffic is moving very slowly. I see a police officer. Police officers make sure that people follow laws. Laws are rules for a community. I'm glad the officer is here.

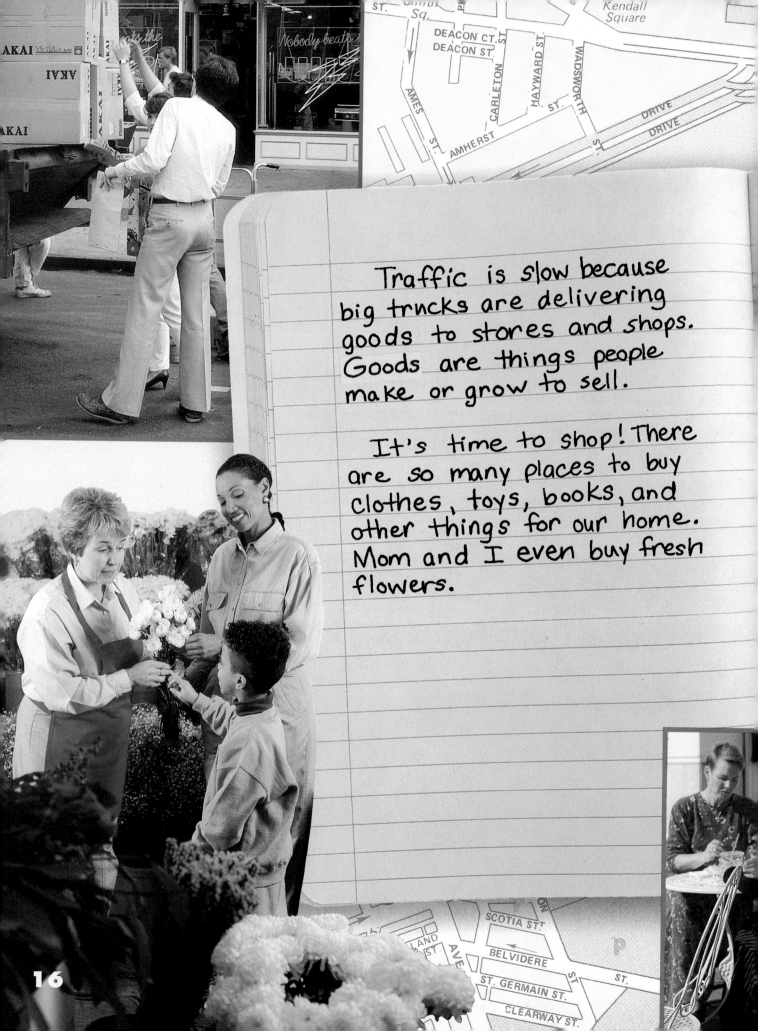

Traffic is slow because big trucks are delivering goods to stores and shops. Goods are things people make or grow to sell.

It's time to shop! There are so many places to buy clothes, toys, books, and other things for our home. Mom and I even buy fresh flowers.

Afternoon

After lunch, Mom and I visit the Computer Museum. A guide tells us about a large computer map. A guide gives a service. Services are jobs that people do for others. I learned a lot from our guide.

Mom and I meet Aunt Leanne for an early dinner. We talk about the fun we had in the busy city. I can't wait until my next visit!

What would you enjoy doing in a city?

17

HOW TO

Read a Map Key

How do you think Jesse and his mom know where to go in the city? Perhaps they read a map. Maps help you find places. A **map key** shows you how to read a map.

1. What is the title of this map?

2. **Symbols** are pictures that stand for things on a map. What symbols are shown in this map key?

3. Find the symbol for the Computer Museum. On what street is the museum located?

4. What is between Bromfield Street and Winter Street near Boston Common?

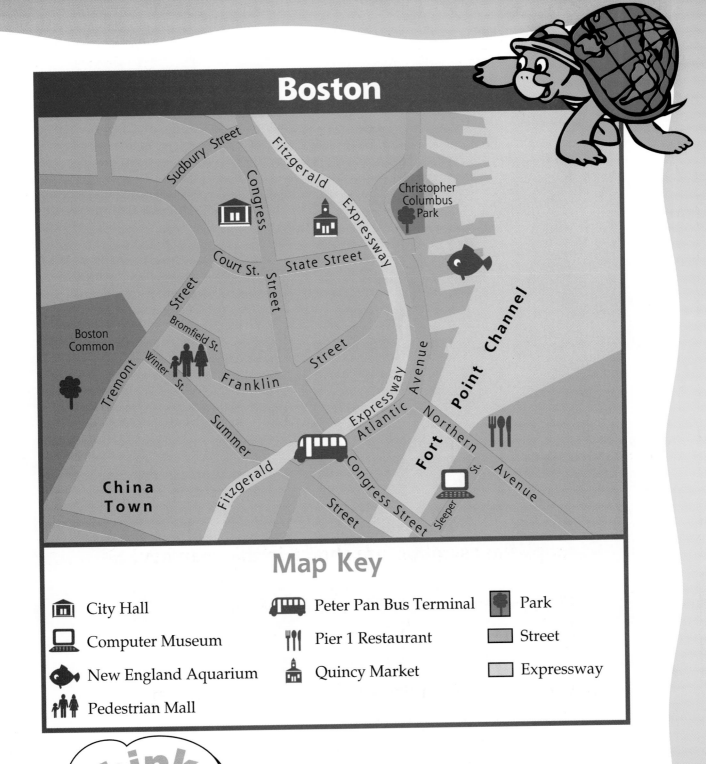

Boston

Map Key

🏛️ City Hall   🚌 Peter Pan Bus Terminal   🌳 Park

💻 Computer Museum   🍴 Pier 1 Restaurant   ▨ Street

🐟 New England Aquarium   ⛪ Quincy Market   ▢ Expressway

👨‍👩‍👧 Pedestrian Mall

Think and Do

Find City Hall. How do you get from City Hall to Christopher Columbus Park? Name some things you pass along the way.

How could you make the park a place
for everyone to enjoy?

•••••••••••••••••••••••••••••••••

Work with some friends. Think of ways to use
the park.

• What special needs does each person have?
• What problems need to be solved?

Show your solution.

● ●

Choose a way to show the class your solution.
- Make a model of the park.
- Write a story.
- Draw a picture.

Our Country of Many People

Our class made a collage of American citizens. **Citizens** are a group of people who belong to a community. We are citizens of our **country**, too. The United States has more than 250 million citizens.

Americans are different in many ways. We live in different places, eat different foods, and hold different jobs. But Americans are alike in special ways. We follow our country's laws. We cooperate, or work together, to make our country a great place to live.

How can you be
a good member of
this large group
of Americans?

23

Story Cloth

Look at the pictures. They will help you remember what you learned.

Talk About the Main Ideas

1. People belong to many groups.
2. Children in school learn together in groups.
3. Families depend on others in the neighborhood.
4. Cities are busy places where people live, work, and play.
5. Communities have laws for order and safety.
6. Our country is home to many different Americans.

Write a List   Many people help you meet your needs. Make a list of some of these people. Tell how you depend on them.

Review

Use Vocabulary

Which word goes with each meaning?

law   goods   services   community   group   map

1. a place where people live, work, and play

2. a drawing that shows where places are

3. a rule that everyone must follow

4. jobs that people do to help others

5. a number of people doing something together

6. things that people make or grow

Check Understanding

1. Name two groups to which you belong.

2. Who are some people in the community on which families depend?

3. How do laws help people in a community? Give an example.

4. In what ways are American citizens different? How are they the same?

Think Critically

1. What might happen if there were no laws in a city?

2. Why should we respect people's differences?

Apply Skills

How to Read a Map and Map Key

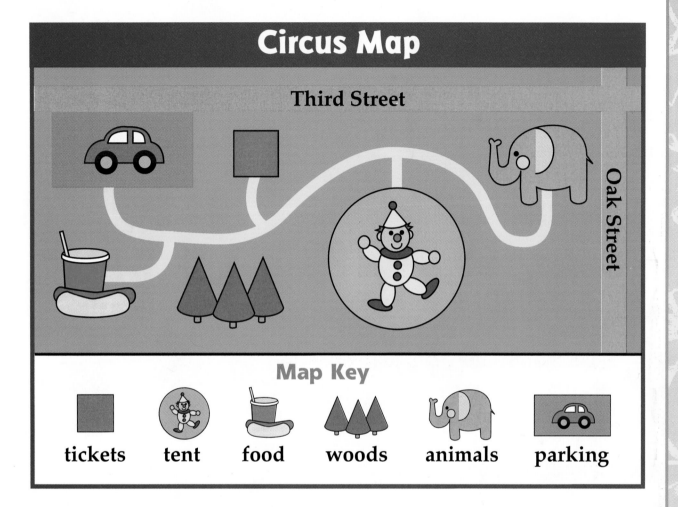

Circus Map

Third Street

Oak Street

Map Key

tickets   tent   food   woods   animals   parking

1. Does the map show the circus from the ground or from the air?

2. What symbol stands for a circus tent?

3. What is between the food area and the animal area?

4. The parking lot is on which street?

Read More About It

Marge's Diner by Gail Gibbons. HarperCollins. Interesting people come into Marge's diner.

Mrs. Katz and Tush by Patricia Polacco. Dell. A young boy helps a neighbor and learns that all people share the same feelings.

Where We Live

geography

continent

landform

28

globe

conservation

resource

Looking Around

by Aileen Fisher

Bees
   own the clover,
birds
   own the sky,
rabbits,
   the meadow
   with low grass and high.

Frogs
   own the marshes,
ants
   own the ground . . .
   I hope they don't mind
   my looking around.

Looking Around Communities

We call what we know about where and how people live **geography**. Look at the photo album that shows the places where people live. They live in communities of different sizes.

Cities are crowded, active places with many things to do. People travel busy streets to live and work in tall buildings.

People can also live in small towns or on farms. Neighbors usually know each other. They sometimes get together to help one another and have fun.

A suburb is a community near a city. Here people live in quiet neighborhoods with less traffic than in cities. Still many people go to work in the city.

You can find different kinds of land near communities. The land can be flat or hilly. The shapes of the land are called **landforms**.

Mountains are the highest kind of land. In some places they are so tall that the snow on top never melts.

Between mountains or hills are lower lands called **valleys**. People may live in the valleys.

Large areas of flat land are called plains. The land found in plains is usually good for farming and raising animals.

Deserts are dry lands that get little rain. They are often hot during the day and cool at night.

People also live around many different bodies of water. Water may be salty or fresh, flowing or still.

Oceans are the largest bodies of water. Their salt water waves fall on beaches in places all over the world.

Some people live on islands in the ocean. An **island** is a landform surrounded on all sides by water.

Bodies of fresh water called **rivers** flow across the land and spill into the oceans. Rivers can flow down mountains and through towns and cities.

Lakes are still bodies of water surrounded by land. Fresh water and salt water lakes are many different sizes.

What pictures would you see in your photo album?

HOW TO

Find Land and Water on a Map

Maps can use colors and symbols to show different kinds of land and bodies of water.

1. Look at the map key. What color are deserts?

2. Use the map key to find the symbol for mountains. Which ocean is near the side of the country that has more mountains?

3. Find lakes and rivers on the map. Which body of water flows between the United States and Mexico? Which bodies of water are found between Canada and the United States?

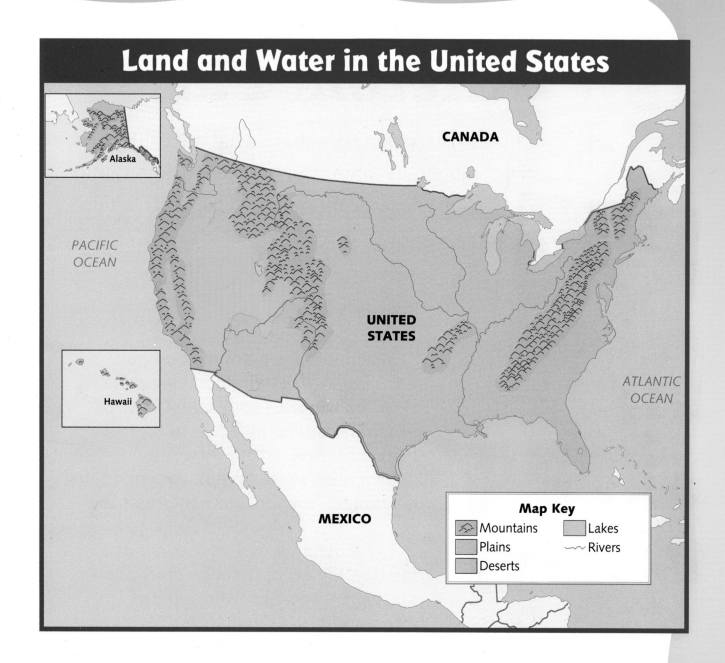

Land and Water in the United States

Alaska

PACIFIC
OCEAN

Hawaii

CANADA

UNITED
STATES

MEXICO

ATLANTIC
OCEAN

Map Key
Mountains Lakes
Plains ~~ Rivers
Deserts

Think and Do

Where are our country's longest rivers? How do you think they help the land?

39

Life in Different Places

Three pen pals share what life is like in a mountain community, an island community, and a desert community. Read their letters.

Dear Felicia,

Hi. I'm glad you are my new pen pal. I live in West Virginia. My house is in the woods. I took a picture of two raccoons in a tree in my backyard. Aren't they cute? It snows a lot in the mountains near my house. Does it snow in Grenada?

My mother works at an animal shelter. My grandfather works at the railroad in town. I like to swim and fish with my friends in the summer. In the winter we enjoy skiing. What do you do for fun?

Your pal,
Jared

Dear Jared,

I live on a small island. I like to fish, too. My family has a fishing farm. On Saturdays I help my father and my uncle on our boat.

Last week we had a big carnival in our town. Almost everybody came. Do you like my costume? My sister painted my face for the parade.

I took a picture of some of my friends at school. It is warm here all the time. I've never even seen snow! What does it feel like? Please write soon.

Your friend,

Felicia

P.S. April is my other pen pal. She is writing you a letter, too.

Dear Jared,

I live with my grandparents in the Cochiti Pueblo in New Mexico. We live in an adobe house. It is very dry here.

Our class went on a field trip. We saw the place where our people lived a long time ago. Their houses were built into the side of the mountain.

My grandparents make beautiful pottery and sell it to visitors. I help them make the pots and dolls out of clay.

Pueblo Feast Day is a special day. Everyone wears a costume. We all dance and sing. Maybe you and Felicia can come feast with us one day. That would be fun! Please write.

Your friend,

April ✓

What would you write in a letter about where you live?

How To

Use a Globe

The places you just read about are in North America. North America is a large land area called a **continent**. You can see continents and oceans on a globe. A **globe** is a model of the Earth.

1. Look at the picture of the globe. How does a globe look like the Earth? How is a globe different from a map?

2. Now look below at the drawings of a globe. How many continents do you see? Name them.

3. How many oceans do you see? Name them.

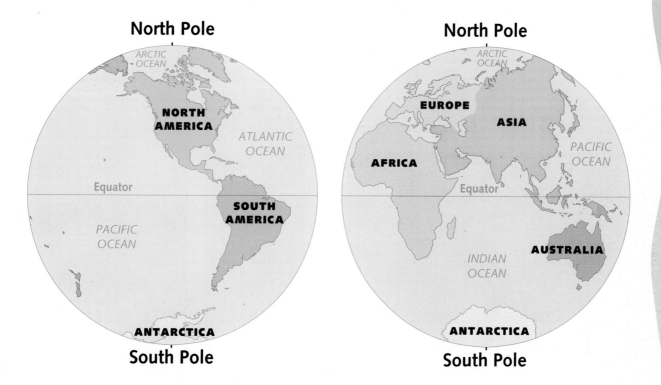

4. Find the North Pole and South Pole on each drawing. Then put your finger on the line drawn halfway between the two poles. This is the **equator**. It is a make-believe line that divides the Earth in half.

Find the equator on a globe. Which three continents does the equator cross?

Using the Land

The children in Jason's class brought pictures and other things from home to help them tell about their families. Jason told the class the story of how his family has used and changed the land on their farm.

Clearing the land

Harvest time

Plowing the field

A long time ago, our farm was covered with trees. My great-grandfather cut down the trees so he could farm the land. A company used the trees to make paper and wood products.

My great-grandfather worked on the farm every day. He worked from early in the morning until it was dark. First, he plowed the field to get it ready for planting. In the spring, he planted the seeds in the warm, soft soil. Farming was very hard work.

Rain and sunshine helped the wheat grow tall. In autumn, the crop was ready to be harvested. All the workers helped cut the wheat. Everyone celebrated at harvest time!

Harvesting wheat on our farm

My family

Farming is different for our family now. But it is still hard work. My father works on the farm every day. We have computers and new machines to help us do our work.

My mother has a job at the television station. She tells about the weather. It is very important for farmers to know when it is going to rain.

Our whole family works hard during planting and harvest time. Harvest time is the best time of the year!

I like to watch while the machine pours the wheat into trucks. The wheat is dried and stored in buildings. Then we sell the grain. Companies use the wheat to make flour, bread, and pasta.

I love living and working on the farm with my family. But my favorite part of farming is sharing the wonderful foods we get from our land.

Loading the grain

How do people use or change the land near you?

LEARN
with
LITERATURE

Focus on resources

How to Make an Apple Pie and see the world

by Marjorie Priceman

The earth gives us many resources. **Resources** are things people use to make what they need. Find out how you can use the whole world as a supermarket.

$\mathcal{M}$aking a pie is really very easy. First, get all the ingredients at the market. Mix them well, bake, and serve. Unless, of course, the market is closed.

In that case, go home and pack a suitcase. Take your shopping list and some walking shoes. Then catch a steamship bound for Europe. Use the six days on board to brush up on your Italian.

If you time it right, you'll arrive in Italy at harvest time. Find a farm deep in the countryside. Gather some superb semolina wheat. An armful or two will do.

Then hop a train to France and locate a chicken.

French chickens lay elegant eggs—and you want only the finest ingredients for your pie. Coax the chicken to give you an egg. Better yet, bring the chicken with you. There's less chance of breaking the egg that way.

Get to Sri Lanka any way you can.

You can't miss it. Sri Lanka is a pear-shaped island in the Indian Ocean. The best cinnamon in the world is made there, from the bark of the native kurundu tree. So go directly to the rain forest. Find a kurundu tree and peel off some bark. If a leopard is napping beneath the tree, be very quiet.

Hitch a ride to England. Make the acquaintance of a cow. You'll know she's an English cow from her good manners and charming accent. Ask her if you can borrow a cup or two of milk. Even better, bring the whole cow with you for the freshest possible results.

Stow away on a banana boat headed home to Jamaica. On your way there, you can pick up some salt. Fill a jar with salty seawater.

When the boat docks in Jamaica, walk to the nearest sugar plantation. Introduce yourself to everyone. Tell them about the pie you're making. Then go into the fields and cut a few stalks of sugar cane.

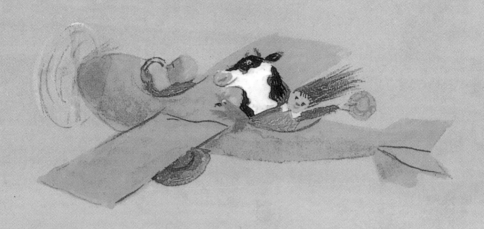

Better fly home. You don't want the ingredients to spoil.

Wait a minute. Aren't you forgetting something? WHAT ABOUT THE APPLES? Have the pilot drop you off in Vermont.

You won't have to go far to find an apple orchard. Pick eight rosy apples from the top of the tree. Give one to the chicken, one to the cow, and eat one yourself. That leaves five for the pie. Then hurry home.

Now all you have to do is
mill the wheat into flour,

grind the kurundu
bark into cinnamon,

evaporate the seawater
from the salt,

boil the sugar cane,

persuade the chicken
to lay an egg,

milk the cow,

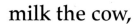

churn the milk
into butter,

slice the apples,

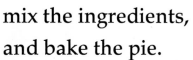

mix the ingredients,
and bake the pie.

While the pie is cooling, invite some
friends over to share it with you.

Remember that apple pie is delicious topped
with vanilla ice cream, which you can get at the
market. But if the market happens to be closed . . .

HOW TO

Read a Table

In How to Make an Apple Pie and see the world, you read about things we use from the Earth. You can use a kind of list called a table to find out about other important resources.

1. Read the title of the table. What does this table show?

2. What four resources are listed on the table?

3. Name two goods made from wheat.

Think and Do

Some goods are listed more than once on the table. What goods are made with more than one resource?

Goods Made from Resources

Resources	Goods			
trees	furniture	books	medicines	tools
oil	fuel	plastics	curtains	medicines
wheat	flour	cereal	pasta	pet food
iron	clips	fire hydrant	pipes	tools

LESSON

Caring for the Earth

My name is Nikko and I love trees. I have the largest leaf collection in my second-grade class. Last week, I interviewed a park ranger named Mia Monroe. She talked to me about conservation.

Conservation is what we must do to protect the forest. Here are some things I found out about being a park ranger.

Nikko: Where do you work?

Ranger Monroe: I work at a national park. A national park is a place where the land and animals are protected. Visitors may see many kinds of plants, animals, and trees.

64

Nikko: What do you like best about being a ranger?

Ranger Monroe: My favorite duty is telling children about the plants and wildlife in the forest.

Nikko: What are your other duties?

Ranger Monroe: I look for people and animals that might be hurt or need help. I collect water and soil samples to test. I also make sure that people are obeying the rules of the forest.

Nikko: What are some of the rules of the forest?

Ranger Monroe: People are not allowed to litter, pick flowers, or cut down trees. They are not allowed to tease or harm the animals. The rules protect the parks so everyone can enjoy them.

Nikko: What tools do you use in your job?

Ranger Monroe: I use maps, a compass, binoculars, and a two-way radio to help me watch the forest.

In my interview, I also learned that park rangers watch for fires in fire towers. These towers stand high above the tree tops. The rangers look for any hint of smoke as they watch over the forest.

It is important for visitors and park rangers to work together to keep the park clean and safe.

Nikko

What questions do you have about taking care of the Earth?

Tree Musketeers

Can kids make a difference? You bet they can! My name is Sabrina. I live in El Segundo, California. My friend and I wanted to help keep the land and water clean. We started a group called Tree Musketeers when we were 8 years old.

The Tree Musketeers decided to try to solve a big problem. El Segundo is next to Los Angeles Airport. There is a lot of noise and air pollution in our town because of the airplanes.

We learned that trees could help stop the pollution from coming into El Segundo. We planted a tree and named it Marcie the Marvelous Tree. We have planted more than 700 trees in El Segundo.

What Can You Do?

- **Make a poster to show something you can do to help the Earth.**
- **Read books about the Earth such as <u>Michael Bird-Boy</u> by Tomie dePaola and <u>A Tree Is Nice</u> by Janice Udry.**

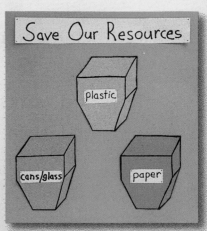

Story Cloth

Look at the pictures. They will help you remember what you learned.

Talk About the Main Ideas

1. Communities are different sizes.
2. Suburbs are close to cities.
3. The Earth has many kinds of land and water.
4. People change the land.
5. People in towns and on farms depend on each other.
6. Important resources come from the Earth.

Describe a Character   Think of a character who might live in the story cloth. Tell where the person lives and works. Tell what the person does for fun.

Review

Use Vocabulary

Choose two words from this list. Write sentences using the words to tell something about where you live.

conservation

continent

geography

globe

landform

resource

Check Understanding

1. How is a suburb different from a city?
2. Name and tell about one landform and one body of water.
3. How do people change the land?
4. Why is water important?
5. Tell about something you use from the land.

Think Critically

1. How does geography help you learn about people?
2. How can you help take care of the Earth? Why is this important?

A. How to Read a Table

Trees		
Kind	**Size**	**Goods**
Maple	50-80 feet	syrup, furniture, musical instruments, boxes
Pecan	90-120 feet	nuts, flooring, furniture, paneling
Pine	75-200 feet	lumber, turpentine, paint, soap, paper
Oak	40-90 feet	lumber, furniture, barrels, railroad ties, paper
Redwood	200-275 feet	home siding, furniture

1. How many kinds of trees are shown on the table?
2. Which tree grows the tallest?
3. What tree gives us syrup?

B. How to Use a Globe

Look at a globe and answer these questions.

1. Is Europe north or south of the equator?
2. What pole is in Antarctica?

Read More About It

Climbing Kansas Mountains by George Shannon. Bradbury. A father and son share the special place where they live.

Radio Man by Arthur Dorros. HarperCollins. Diego goes with his family from farm to farm. He helps pick fruit and vegetables.

People Make History

VOCABULARY

history

settler

landmark

President

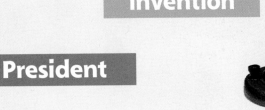

invention

I Can

by Mari Evans

I can
be anything
I can
do anything
I can
think
anything
big
or tall
OR
high or low
WIDE
or narrow
fast or slow
because I
CAN
and
I
WANT
TO!

We Remember the Past

The **history** of a country is the story of people and happenings over time. Compare daily life in early America with the way you live.

Many years ago people came to live in America from other countries. These early American **settlers** built their own houses and grew their own food. They burned wood to cook food and heat their cabins. Families dried, smoked, and salted some foods to store them for the winter. How does your family store food?

Getting clothing was a lot more work back then! Early Americans sheared sheep for wool. They spun wool into thread. Then they wove the thread into cloth on a loom and made the cloth into clothing. How does your family get the clothes you need?

Most towns printed a newspaper. The newspaper was a very important way for people to learn about their community and the world. How do people get news today?

Early American settlers enjoyed some of the same activities we do. They played games with their friends. Families spent time together.

Could the early American settlers do what you like to do? Why or why not?

HOW TO
Read a Time Line

July	August	September

July 22
**Pilgrims sail from the
Netherlands to England**

September 16
**Mayflower sails
for America**

A **time line** shows the order in which things happened. This time line tells the story of the Pilgrims. They were early settlers who came to America.

1. How much time is shown on the time line?

2. In what month did the <u>Mayflower</u> leave for America?

3. In November the Pilgrims signed a plan for ruling the new settlement. What was it called?

October	November	December

November 21
Mayflower Compact is signed

December 25
Plymouth is chosen as new home

Think and Do

How many months before the <u>Mayflower</u> landed the Pilgrims at Plymouth?

Communities Grow and Change

San Antonio is a very old city in Texas. Join Miguel as he learns how the city has changed and grown.

Miguel: How old is our city, Grandpa?

Grandpa: San Antonio began way back in 1718 as a Spanish fort. Father Antonio Olivarez and other people from Spain built several churches here called missions.

Mission San José was built in 1720. It is called the "Queen of the Missions" because it is so beautiful. This mission is a landmark in San Antonio. A **landmark** is something people easily see and know as part of the community.

Miguel: The Alamo must be a landmark, too.

Grandpa: Yes, Miguel. The Alamo was built as a mission when San Antonio began. When more people came to San Antonio, the Alamo was used as a hospital and a place for soldiers to live.

The Alamo played a big part in Texas history. Nearly two hundred Americans and Mexicans fought and died there in the Texas Revolution. That was when Texas was still part of Mexico. Texas became part of the United States in 1845.

ANDREW KENT · JOSEPH KERR · GEORGE C. KIMBLE · WILLIAM P. KING · JOHN G. KING · WILLIAM IRVINE LEWIS · WI
JAMES MCGEE · ROBERT MCKINNEY · ELIEL MELTON · THOMAS R. MILLER · WILLIAM MILLS · ISAAC MILLSAPS
JAMES NOWLAN · GEORGE PAGAN · CHRISTOPHER A. PARKER · JUAN ANTONIO PADILLO · WILLIAM PA
OLELLAND KINLOCH SIMMONS · ANDREW H. SMITH · CHARLES S. SMITH · JOSHUA G. SMITH · WILLIA
JOHN W. THOMSON · JOHN M. THRUSTON · BURKE TRAMMEL · WILLIAM BARRET TRAVIS · GEORGE W. TUMLIN

Grandpa: Many people in San Antonio have a Spanish or Mexican background. This painting along Riverwalk shows pride in our history.

Miguel: This part of our city is new and modern.

Grandpa: Yes, Miguel. People come here to enjoy the shops, hotels, and cafes along the San Antonio River.

When I was a boy, this river flooded much of the city. Then San Antonio was built again even better than before. It is still growing and changing.

San Antonio is much more than a little village now. It is one of the largest cities in the United States. Many people work at the factories, hospitals, and military bases here. There are many things to see and do in our city.

Miguel: San Antonio is a good place to visit and a good place to live.

What are some landmarks in your community?

SKILLS
How To
Find Cause and Effect

Changes happen for different reasons. What makes something happen is a cause. What happens is an effect.

1. Look at the first picture. This was San Antonio long ago. What was the community like?

2. Look at the picture below. What changes do you see?

3. Why do you think San Antonio grew?

Think and Do

What do you think caused the railroad to come to San Antonio?

People Lead the Way

Washington, D.C., is our nation's capital. A **capital** is a city where the leaders of a country work. Come along as we tour this special city.

Here is the White House where the President lives. The **President** is the leader of the United States. Many Presidents have lived in the White House since it was built in 1800. This building has been changed many times. Our country has changed, too.

TOUR GUIDE

This is the Capitol Building where the lawmakers work. **Lawmakers** are people who make the laws of our country. The Capitol Building has had three different domes. The dome is a symbol of our country's greatness.

The **Congress** is the group of lawmakers who work in the Capitol Building. They are some of the leaders who help our country grow and change. They plan ways to keep our country healthy and strong.

Jefferson Memorial

Lincoln
Memorial

This popular part of the city is called the
West Mall. But it is not for shopping. People
come here to see the monuments. They are
places or buildings built to honor someone.
The Washington Monument and the Lincoln
and Jefferson memorials honor three great
Presidents. Each of these men helped lead
our country through hard times.

Washington Monument

92

People also visit Arlington National Cemetery and the Vietnam Veterans Memorial. These places honor men and women who have died for our country. There are many special places in our country's capital.

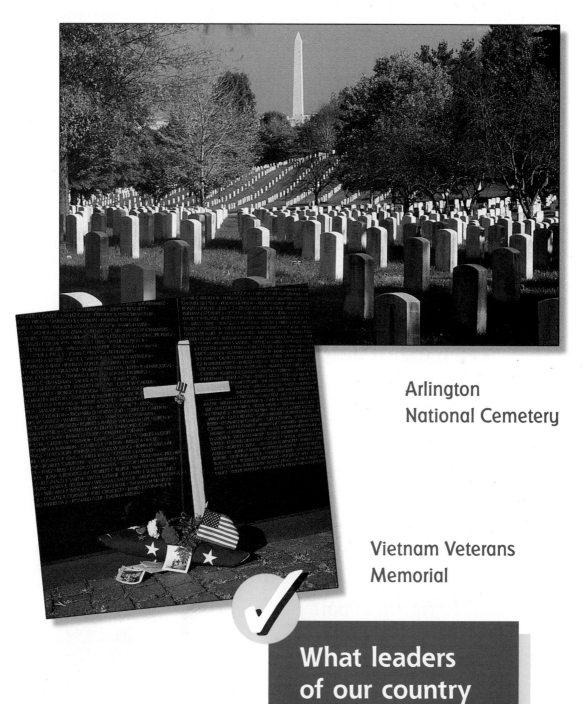

Arlington National Cemetery

Vietnam Veterans Memorial

What leaders of our country can you name?

93

HOW TO

Use a Map Grid

Visitors to Washington, D.C., often use maps to find the shortest route. A **route** is a way to travel from one place to another. To help you find places, this map has a set of squares called a **grid**. Each grid square has a number and a letter.

1. Find the Lincoln Memorial. It is in square B-1. In which square is the Washington Monument?

2. In which square is the Vietnam Veterans Memorial?

3. What is in square E-5?

4. In which squares is the Reflecting Pool?

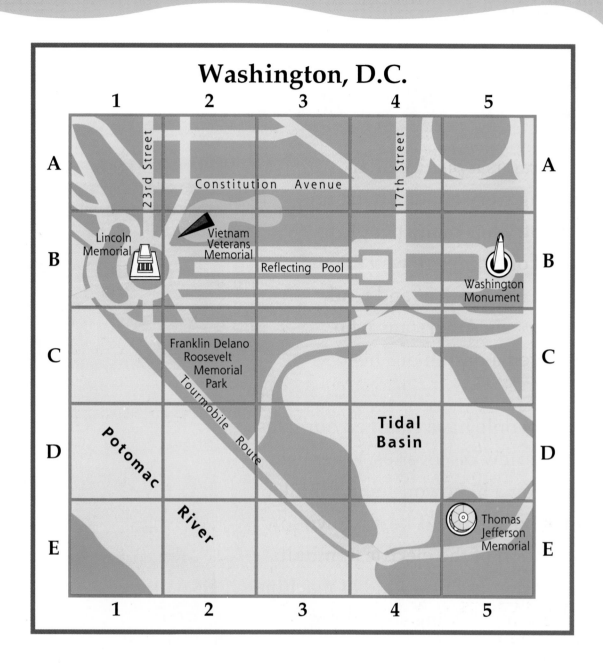

Washington, D.C.

Think and Do

Follow a route. Put your finger in square E-5. Travel up to C-5. Go left to C-2. What park is in the center of the square?

American Portraits

A portrait is a picture or an interesting story about a person. Our country has many people to be proud of. Some are well known. Some are not. Look at and read portraits of six Americans who have played a part in our history.

Some people have changed our lives with their new discoveries. Whenever you turn on a light, you should think of Thomas Edison. He is best known for his invention of the electric lightbulb. An **invention** is a new kind of machine or a new way of doing something. Edison also invented the phonograph. He became known as the "Wizard of Menlo Park." Menlo Park is where he worked.

Like scientists, other leaders have helped change the lives of Americans. Sam Houston was an army leader. At one time he was even president of a country! Texas was a country before he helped it to join the United States. After Texas became a state, Texans chose Sam Houston to go to Washington, D.C., to work in Congress. Sam Houston worked hard for the people of his state and for the whole country.

More than 150 years after Sam Houston, Barbara Jordan became a leader who also served her state and her country. She was a lawyer and a teacher. She was the first African American woman chosen to be in the Texas Senate. Later, the people of Texas chose her to work in the United States Congress. In all her jobs Barbara Jordan spoke about being fair and serving others. She helped people see that everyone can help make the world a better place.

Some people speak out when laws are unfair. Susan B. Anthony spoke out. She was a teacher who said that our country's laws should be for all Americans. During her life only men could vote. Her work helped change laws so that women could vote, too. Anthony was the first woman on American money. Her picture is on the silver dollar.

Dr. Martin Luther King, Jr., also worked for the fair treatment of all Americans. We honor his hard work with a holiday to celebrate his birthday.

Dr. King was a minister. He believed that people should not be treated differently because of their skin color. Dr. King was a powerful speaker. Many people followed his peaceful message for change. Later they were shocked and sad when Dr. King was shot. Today, people still remember his message.

Many years ago, a Cherokee named Sequoyah wanted to help his people learn. Yet his people did not have an alphabet. He decided to change that.

One day, Sequoyah wrote down some words whispered to him by a stranger. He passed the paper to his daughter Ahyoka sitting far away. Ahyoka read the words. The Cherokee were amazed at the "talking leaves." Not only did Sequoyah invent an alphabet, but it was then used to write a newspaper for his people. His great invention helped the Cherokee people learn more and more.

Whose portrait would you add to this list of important Americans?

Brainstorm

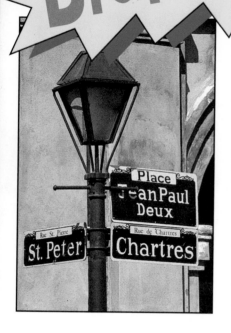

What can the pictures tell you about history?

Work with a group.

Make a list of the clues you see.

- How might each picture give you a clue about history?
- Which are the easiest clues to understand?
- What other clues can you think of?

Show your ideas.

● ●

Choose a way to show the class your ideas.

- Invent a story about the meaning of one of the clues.

- Do a role-play solving a history mystery.

- Draw a picture of some other clues to history.

Story Cloth

Follow the pictures. They will help you remember what you learned.

Talk About the Main Ideas

1. American Indians were the earliest people living in and caring for our country.
2. Settlers from other countries built new homes in America.
3. Important leaders have shaped our history.
4. Communities grow and change.
5. Many different kinds of people make America great.

Write About a Hero Choose someone you like. Write why you think that person is important. Tell what you can learn from your hero.

Review

Use Vocabulary

Which word best fits the sentence?

settler   invention   President   landmark   history

1. One way to learn about the past is to read _____ books.

2. You can read about _____ Abraham Lincoln.

3. You can also read about the hard life of an early American _____.

4. You can learn about Thomas Edison's _____ of the lightbulb.

5. You can also learn about the Alamo or another _____ of interest.

Check Understanding

1. How was the life of an American settler different from your life?

2. What can cause a community to change?

3. Who makes the laws for our country, and where do they work?

4. Name an invention and tell how it has changed people's lives.

Think Critically

1. What is history, and why do we study it?

2. Why are monuments and landmarks important to people in a community?

Apply Skills

A. How to Use a Map Grid

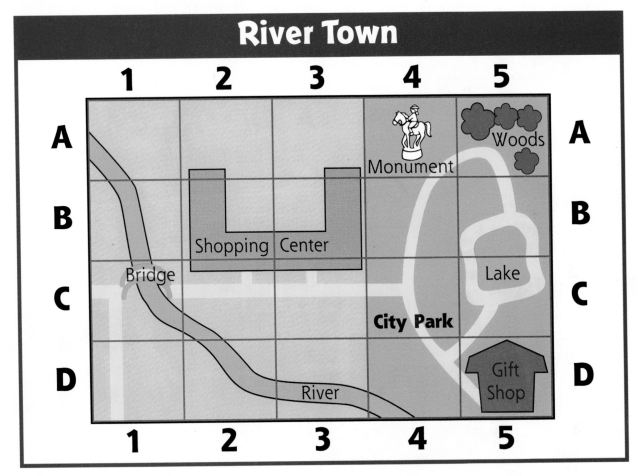

River Town

1. What building is in D-5?
2. In which square is the monument?
3. How many squares are between the park and the bridge?

B. How to Read a Time Line

Make a time line to show when people in your family have birthdays.

Read More About It

<u>The Joke's on George</u> by Michael O. Tunnell. Tambourine. George Washington visits a friend's museum.

<u>McGraw's Emporium</u> by Jim Aylesworth. Henry Holt. Mr. McGraw's store is packed with things from different countries and different times.

We All Work Together

VOCABULARY

taxes

TAX COLLECTOR

transportation

factory

106

producer

consumer

income

107

GENERAL STORE

by Rachel Field

Some day I'm going to have a store

With a tinkly bell hung over the door,

With real glass cases and counters wide

And drawers all spilly with things inside.

There'll be a little of everything;

Bolts of calico; balls of string;

Jars of peppermint; tins of tea;

Pots and kettles and crockery;

Seeds in packets; scissors bright;

Kegs of sugar, brown and white;

Sarsaparilla for picnic lunches;

Bananas and rubber boots in bunches.

I'll fix the window and dust each shelf,

And take the money in all myself,

It will be my store and I will say:

"What can I do for you today?"

Community Services

My class has been learning about how a community pays for its services. We read this article in our weekly news magazine.

Taxes Pay for Community Services

Communities collect money from people who live there. This money is called **taxes**. Some of the taxes are used to pay the workers. Tax money pays teachers, police officers, and firefighters. This money pays our community leaders, too.

Taxes are used to build schools and to buy police cars and fire trucks. Taxes pay for the care children get at health clinics. Tax money helps a community take care of its citizens.

> **Tax money helps a community take care of its citizens.**

How do taxes help your community?

111

SKILLS

HOW TO

Use a Pictograph

Mr. Lee's class made a pictograph to show the places that give services in their community. A **pictograph** uses pictures to show numbers of things.

1. Look at the pictograph. How many services are shown?

2. Find the Key. What symbol is used to show the number of places that give each kind of service?

3. Find the school. How many schools are there? Count the symbols to find out.

4. Find the fire station. Are there more or fewer fire stations than schools?

Services in Our Community

Bank	🏢 🏢 🏢
Fire Station	🏢 🏢 🏢
Hospital	🏢
Post Office	🏢 🏢
School	🏢 🏢 🏢 🏢
Key	🏢 = 1 service

Think and Do

Think of another service you could add to the pictograph.

People Make Goods

Last week Josh's class went on a field trip. Follow their tour to see what they learned about how sneakers are made.

1. Sneaker factories are very busy places. A **factory** is a place where goods are made. Each factory worker has a special job to do.

2. Rubber is shipped from countries that are far away. The rubber is melted into molds to shape the sneaker bottoms.

3. Machines cut out the top parts of the sneakers, and workers sew the parts together.

4. Workers punch holes into the shoes for the laces. Then, they glue the tops and bottoms together.

5. Next, they glue rubber strips around the sneakers.

6. Finally, the shoes are placed on a rack to be baked in an oven. This makes them strong.

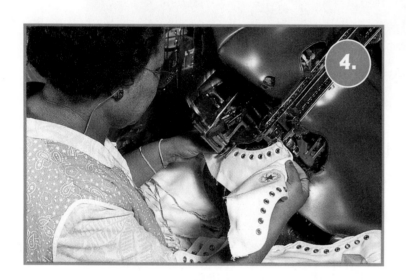

7. When the sneakers are ready, workers slip laces through the holes. Then the shoes are put in boxes. The boxes are packed onto trucks and sent to stores.

Look at your shoes. Can you tell how they were made?

How To

Predict a Likely Outcome

New Shoes

Kim got money from her aunt and uncle on her birthday. "Thank you," she said. "I'll use it to buy a new pair of shoes."

At the store, the shoe seller asked Kim, "What kind of shoes are you looking for?"

Kim said, "All my friends are wearing bright-colored sneakers. I want pink ones!"

"I am sorry," said the shoe seller. "We have only black and white sneakers. How would you like a nice pair of sandals?"

What do you think will happen next? What will Kim do? What will the shoe seller do?

You are making a **prediction** when you say what you think will happen next. One way to make good predictions is to follow steps.

1. Read the story. Think about what you know about Kim. What does she want to buy?

2. Look for clues in the story. What does the shoe seller want her to do?

3. Think about what will happen next. Make a prediction.

Think and Do

If a sneaker factory cannot get the rubber it needs to make its shoes, what will happen? Make a prediction.

Goods from Near and Far

Countries all over the world trade goods. To **trade** means to buy and sell things. The United States sells cotton, clothing, and food to countries such as China and Mexico. We buy cameras and machines from countries such as Japan and Germany.

Countries use many kinds of **transportation** to move goods. Goods travel by trains, planes, ships, and trucks.

My class has made a catalog of goods we buy from other countries. These goods come from all around the world.

Goods from Other Countries

Look at our class catalog. What are some goods we buy from Mexico, Scotland, and Japan?

People collect pottery from Mexico to decorate their homes.

Wool sweaters from Scotland keep people warm in cold weather.

WOOL

Children love to play some computer games made in Japan.

Some countries have special foods, metals, or plants.
Who might want tulips from Holland?

These bananas grew on plants in Costa Rica.

This was made from gold mined in South Africa.

Holland's tulip bulbs grow into beautiful flowers.

Sometimes we buy resources from other countries.
American workers make goods from the resources.
What might they make from these resources?

Chocolate is made from cocoa beans found in Ecuador.

Rubber comes from trees in Malaysia.

Canada has lots of trees that give us lumber.

✔

What goods from other countries can you find in your community?

Makers and Users, Buyers and Sellers

Our school collected money to buy a gift for a sick classmate. Everyone thought of ways to earn money.

Last week our class had an arts and crafts sale. We painted pictures and made clay pots to sell. I sold a picture of my dog, Red, for 25 cents. Our teacher said that we were producers. **Producers** make or grow things to sell.

124

We invited our
families and friends to
the sale. My sister bought two
plants for her room. She was a consumer.
Consumers use things made by producers.

Today the school sent a new computer to
Mandy. The money we earned helped buy the
gift. The computer will make it easier for
Mandy to learn at home.

When are you
a consumer?

Making Wise Choices

Wants are goods and services that people would like to have. People cannot buy everything they want. They must make choices. Read to see how Jarrod plans to spend his money.

I earn money by washing cars for my neighbors. I also do extra chores at home, such as raking leaves. The money I earn is called **income**.

126

I spend some of my income. I keep the money in a bank until I want to spend it. Gran and Pops gave me money on my birthday. I am saving that money for college. I keep it in the bank, too.

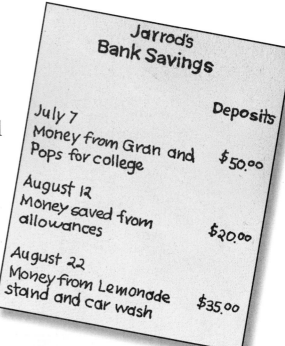

Jarrod's
Bank Savings

Deposits

July 7
Money from Gran and
Pops for college $50.00

August 12
Money saved from
allowances $20.00

August 22
Money from Lemonade
stand and car wash $35.00

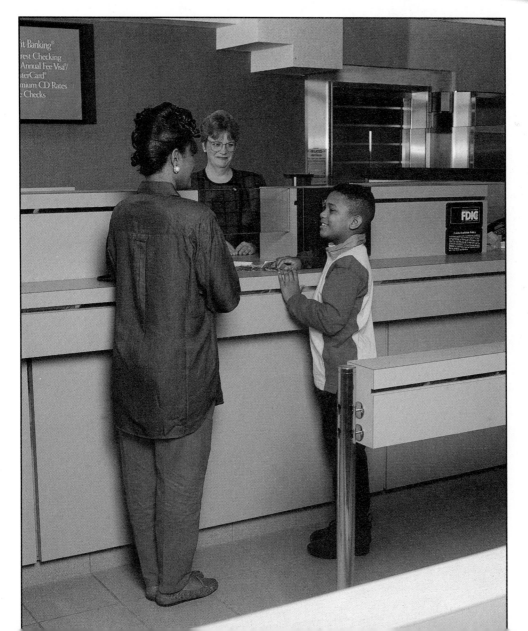

When I shop, I see many things I want to buy. I make choices about how to spend my money. I do not have enough money yet to buy a new bike. And if I buy a fish tank, I will have to buy fish food every week.

I decide to buy a soccer ball. I like to play games with my friends. I will have money left over after I buy the ball. I take the money I think I will need out of the bank.

Mom and I look in different stores. There are many kinds of balls. Some cost more than others. I choose one that is on sale. It has been marked at a lower price to get us to spend our money in that store.

Now I think I made a good choice. I have fun playing soccer with my friends.

What ways do you choose to spend your money?

SKILLS

HOW TO

Follow a Diagram

Have you ever wondered how money is made? A **diagram** is a drawing that shows parts of something or how something is made. This diagram shows the parts of a coin.

reeded ridge

face

U.S. motto

mint date

mint mark

Latin motto (out of many, one)

eagle

Look at a penny, a nickel, and a dime. How are they like the quarter? How are they different?

This diagram shows how coins are minted, or made.

1. A machine traces the model and carves it smaller onto a steel stamp.

2. Bars of metal are rolled into strips and cut into blank coins.

3. A coining press stamps designs on both sides of the coin.

4. A machine counts and bags the coins ready to go to the bank.

Think and Do

Design your own coin or paper money and draw a diagram to show the different parts.

Biz Kid$

One store in Orlando, Florida, is completely run by children. It's called BIZ KID$. Everyone from the greeter to the check-out person is in the fifth grade.

Working at BIZ KID$ is part of a social studies class. The fifth-graders are taught how to greet people, count money, sell goods to customers, use a cash register, and get along with other workers.

Students say that working at BIZ KID$ is a lot of fun, and they learn a lot about business, too. Some of the goods fifth-graders sell are snacks, first-aid supplies, and Earth-friendly products. At the end of the year, the students of each class get to decide how they will spend the money they made.

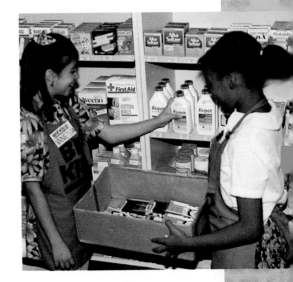

What Can You Do?

- Write to find out more about BIZ KID$.
- Start a class business, and vote on what to do with the money you make.

Story Cloth

Look at the pictures. They will help you remember what you learned.

Talk About the Main Ideas

1. Service workers keep our communities healthy and safe.
2. Workers in factories make many things we need.
3. People trade goods and money for what they want.
4. Producers and consumers depend on each other.
5. People make choices about how to spend their money.

Think and Draw   Think of a job that might interest you someday. Draw a picture that shows the machines or tools you would use.

Review

Use Vocabulary

Which word goes with each box?

consumer   **factory**   **transportation**
producer   **income**   **taxes**

1 train, ship, truck, airplane

2 money someone earns

3 place where things are made

4 farmer, baker, quilt maker

5 buyer and user of products

6 money paid to a community

Check Understanding

1. How do taxes help a community?

2. Why are factories important to people?

3. Why does the United States trade goods with other countries?

4. Name a product we get from another country. Tell where it comes from and how it might get here.

5. What choices must consumers make about spending money?

Think Critically

1. Tell how a producer can also be a consumer.

2. Predict what would happen if people did not pay taxes.

Apply Skills

A. How to Use a Pictograph

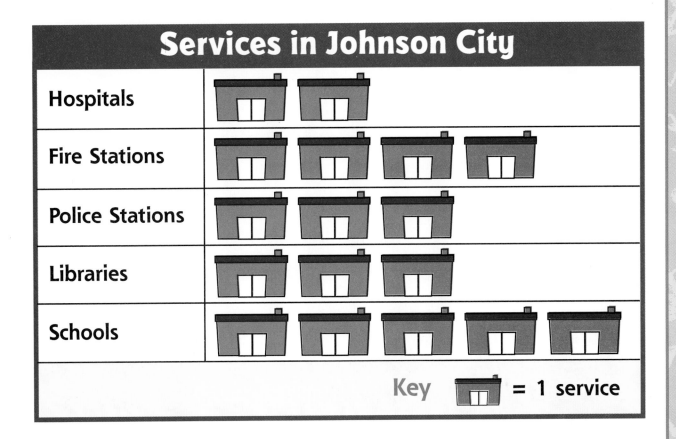

1. What services does Johnson City provide?
2. How many libraries are there?
3. Are there more fire stations or police stations? How many more?

B. How to Follow a Diagram

Draw a diagram to show what you do to get a library book.

Read More About It

We Keep a Store by Anne Shelby. Orchard. Everyone in a family works together to run a country store.

Music, Music for Everyone by Vera B. Williams. Greenwillow. Rosa and her friends start a band that plays at parties. Best of all, they get paid!

Being A Good Citizen

VOCABULARY

vote

government

judge

mayor

freedom

We the People

139

America

by Samuel F. Smith

My country, 'tis of thee,
Sweet land of liberty,
Of thee I sing;

Land where my fathers died,
Land of the pilgrims' pride,
From every mountainside
Let freedom ring.

My native country, thee,
Land of the noble free,
Thy name I love;

I love thy rocks and rills,
Thy woods and templed hills;
My heart with rapture thrills
Like that above.

Proud Americans

The Fourth of July is our country's birthday. Our community celebrates this **holiday** with a parade. Did you know that the United States is more than 200 years old?

United States of America

We like to honor our country during the school year, too. We decorate our room with balloons. We hang a banner of our country's motto, In God We Trust. A **motto** is a saying that people try to live by.

E Pluribus Unum is a motto that is printed on our money. The Latin words mean "out of many, one." We are one country of many different people.

142

Our country has many symbols. My class is making a bulletin board. We will show pictures of our country's symbols, such as the Statue of Liberty and the White House. Cao is drawing a picture of another symbol, the North American bald eagle.

Ms. Carroll's class is having a play. The children in the play are dressed as people in American history. They tell us about other American symbols.

I am Betsy Ross.

I sewed the first American flag. Our flag is red, white, and blue. Each star stands for one of the states in our country. The stripes stand for the first 13 states in the United States.

I am Francis Scott Key.

I wrote our country's anthem. An anthem is a special song. The anthem of the United States is about the American flag. Can you sing "The Star-Spangled Banner"?

My name is George Washington.

I was the first President of the United States. You can see my picture and the Great Seal of the United States on a one-dollar bill. The Great Seal is on important papers, too.

I am Thomas Jefferson.

In 1776 I wrote the Declaration of Independence that helped start the United States. People showed their love for the new country by ringing the Liberty Bell every Fourth of July. In 1835 the Liberty Bell cracked.

How do you show pride in your country?

SKILLS
HOW TO
Make a Choice by Voting

Leaders in our country, like Washington and Jefferson, are chosen in an **election**. Here is how it works.

Today is election day at Lincoln Elementary School. Each class will choose someone to send to a special student meeting. In an election, people **vote** to choose the person who will speak for them.

1. When people vote, they think about who will do the best job. What choice do these children have?

2. One way to vote is to mark a piece of paper called a ballot. Each person has only one vote. How does the girl in the picture show her choice? Why does she mark only one name on the ballot?

3. How will the children decide who wins?

4. All voters agree to accept the winner.

Make a list of the reasons you would vote for someone in an election.

Our Country's Government

My class is learning about the people who make laws and lead our country. These groups of people are our government.

The Constitution is the highest law in our country. It protects all the people of the United States. The Constitution tells about the three branches, or parts, of our government. Each branch has its own job to do. We are making a mobile to show the branches of our government.

The President's office is one branch of our government. The President leads our country. The President chooses people to help and to give advice. They work together in the White House. Do you know the name of our President?

Congress is another branch of government. Members of Congress make new laws. These lawmakers come from communities all over the country. They vote for the laws they think we need.

The Supreme Court is also a branch of our government. It is the highest court in the United States. A court is where judges work. Judges tell us whether laws are fair and whether laws have been broken.

There are nine judges in the Supreme Court. They are called justices. Sandra Day O'Connor is the first woman to be a Supreme Court justice.

The President, the Congress, and the Supreme Court are in Washington, D.C. All three branches of the government work together to lead our country.

Why do you think it is important to have good leaders?

HOW TO

Find Directions on a Map

Our country has fifty states. The map of the United States on the next page shows the boundary of each state. A **boundary** is the line around a state. It tells where the state begins and ends. Each state also has a capital city for its own government.

1. Look at the map key. What symbol stands for a state capital? Find your state on the map. What is its capital city? What is the name of our country's capital?

2. Find the compass rose in the center at the bottom of the map. A **compass rose** gives us directions on a map. The four main **directions** are north, south, east, and west.

3. Point to your state on the map. Tell what is north, south, east, and west of your state.

152

United States

Map Key
⊛ National capital — Boundary
★ State capital

RUSSIA
ARCTIC OCEAN
ALASKA
CANADA
Juneau
PACIFIC OCEAN

CANADA

Olympia ★
WASHINGTON
★ Salem
OREGON
★ Boise
IDAHO
★ Helena
MONTANA
NORTH DAKOTA
★ Bismarck
MINNESOTA
St. Paul
SOUTH DAKOTA
★ Pierre
WISCONSIN
★ Madison
Lake Superior
MICHIGAN
Lake Huron
Lansing ★
Lake Michigan
Lake Ontario
Lake Erie
NEW HAMPSHIRE
VERMONT
★ Montpelier
MAINE
★ Augusta
★ Concord
NEW YORK
★ Albany
★ Boston
MASSACHUSETTS
RHODE ISLAND
★ Providence
Hartford ★
CONNECTICUT

Sacramento ★
★ Carson City
NEVADA
★ Salt Lake City
UTAH
WYOMING
Cheyenne ★
Denver ★
COLORADO
NEBRASKA
Lincoln ★
IOWA
Des Moines
ILLINOIS
Springfield ★
INDIANA
Indianapolis ★
OHIO
Columbus ★
PENNSYLVANIA
Harrisburg ★
Annapolis ★
WEST VIRGINIA
★ Charleston
Trenton ★
NEW JERSEY
★ Dover
DELAWARE
MARYLAND
★ Washington, D.C.
Richmond ★

CALIFORNIA
ARIZONA
★ Phoenix
Santa Fe ★
NEW MEXICO
KANSAS
Topeka ★
MISSOURI
Jefferson City ★
KENTUCKY
Frankfort ★
VIRGINIA
Raleigh ★
NORTH CAROLINA
★ Nashville
TENNESSEE
OKLAHOMA
Oklahoma City ★
ARKANSAS
Little Rock ★
ALABAMA
Atlanta ★
Columbia ★
SOUTH CAROLINA
GEORGIA

PACIFIC OCEAN

TEXAS
Austin ★
LOUISIANA
Jackson ★
MISSISSIPPI
Montgomery ★
Baton Rouge ★
★ Tallahassee
FLORIDA
ATLANTIC OCEAN

★ Honolulu
HAWAII
PACIFIC OCEAN

MEXICO

Gulf of Mexico

N W E S

Think and Do

Find the capital of Indiana. What is the capital of the state east of Indiana? What is the capital of the state west of Indiana?

Community Government

Citizens can work together to make changes. Last year children in our school needed a new playground. We wanted to use an empty lot near the school. Maya's dad helped us write a letter. We asked our teachers, parents, and neighbors to sign it.

Noel's mom gave the letter to the school board. The school board held a meeting. Many people came to the meeting to listen and speak. The school board voted to buy the empty lot.

Citizens worked together to build the playground. The mayor started the job. He is one of our city leaders.

My teacher says we are lucky to live in the United States. Citizens have the freedom to make things happen. We can make changes in our schools, communities, states, and country.

How can you work with your leaders?

SKILLS

HOW TO

Understand What People Think

Not everyone in Maya and Noel's neighborhood wanted a new playground in the empty lot. Read this letter to the school board.

Dear Members of the School Board,

I live in the building next to the empty lot. The lot has been for sale for many months. I know that you want to buy it for a playground. I think that is a bad idea. Children make too much noise. I think they will also leave garbage behind them. I hope you will put your playground somewhere else. Thank you.

Sincerely,

Mr. Wilson

Mr. Wilson

People often have strong feelings about things. They want others to listen to their ideas. Sometimes they tell facts, or true statements. Sometimes they give opinions. Opinions tell what people think. Not everyone has the same opinions.

1. Read Mr. Wilson's letter. What does he feel strongly about?

2. What facts does he give about the empty lot?

3. What opinions does he have about children? How can you tell?

Think and Do

Work with a partner. Write your own letter to the school board. Give two facts and two opinions about why the playground should be built in the empty lot.

Matthew and Tilly

by Rebecca C. Jones   illustrated by Beth Peck

Matthew and Tilly were friends.

They rode bikes together, and they played hide-and-seek together. They sold lemonade together. When business was slow, they played sidewalk games together. And sometimes they ate ice-cream cones together.

Once they even rescued a lady's kitten from a tree together. The lady gave them money for the bubble-gum machines. So later they chewed gum together and remembered how brave they had been.

Sometimes though, Matthew and Tilly got sick of each other. One day when they were coloring, Matthew broke Tilly's purple crayon. He didn't mean to, but he did.

"You broke my crayon," Tilly said in her crabbiest voice.

"It was an old crayon," Matthew said in his grouchiest voice. "It was ready to break."

"No it wasn't," Tilly said. "It was a brand-new crayon, and you broke it. You always break everything."

"Stop being so picky," Matthew said. "You're always so picky and stinky and mean."

"Well you're so stupid," Tilly said. "You're so stupid and stinky and mean."

Matthew stomped up the stairs. By himself. Tilly found a piece of chalk and began drawing numbers and squares on the sidewalk. By herself.

Upstairs, Matthew got out his cash register and some cans so he could play store. He piled the cans extra high, and he put prices on everything. This was the best store he had ever made. Probably because that picky and stinky and mean old Tilly wasn't around to mess it up.

But he didn't have a customer. And playing store wasn't much fun without a customer.

Tilly finished drawing the numbers and squares.
She drew them really big, with lots of squiggly lines.
This was the best sidewalk game she had ever drawn.
Probably because that stupid and stinky and mean old
Matthew wasn't around to mess it up.

But she didn't have anyone to play with. And a
sidewalk game wasn't much fun without another player.

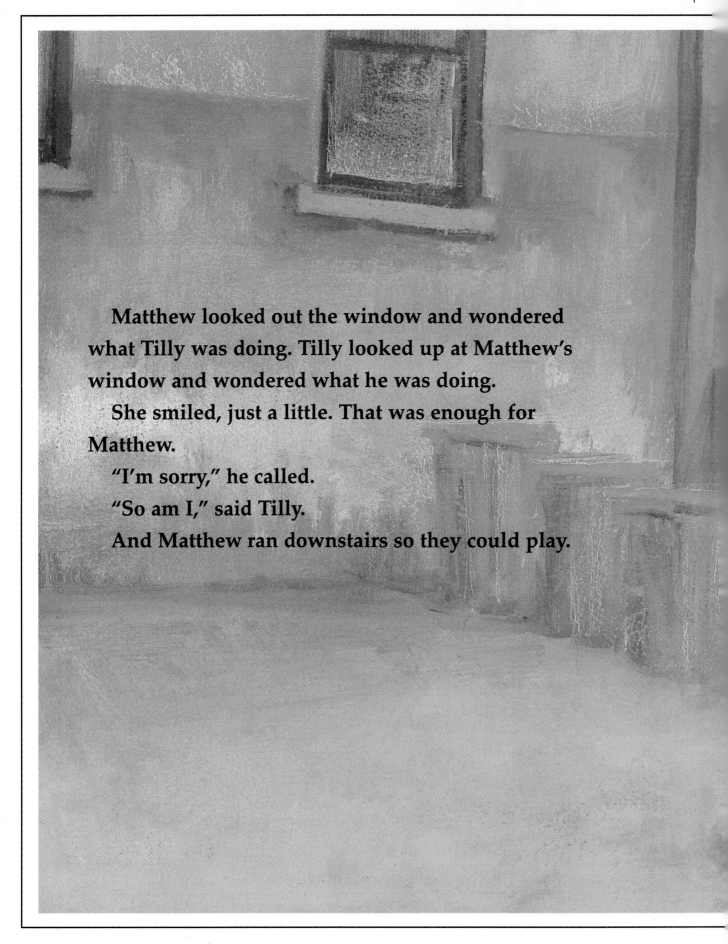

Matthew looked out the window and wondered what Tilly was doing. Tilly looked up at Matthew's window and wondered what he was doing.

She smiled, just a little. That was enough for Matthew.

"I'm sorry," he called.

"So am I," said Tilly.

And Matthew ran downstairs so they could play.

Together again.

How did Matthew and Tilly become friends again?

Brainstorm

Who's right and who's wrong?

• •

Work with a group.

Talk about the children's different opinions.

- Why does each child think he or she is right?
- How can the children settle their fight?

What would you do?

Choose a way to show the class your ideas.

- Draw a cartoon.
- Act out your way to solve the problem.
- Write a story.

Story Cloth

Look at the pictures. They will help you remember what you learned.

Talk About the Main Ideas

1. Americans treasure their country and its history.
2. We elect people to help us govern our country.
3. The United States government has three branches.
4. States and communities have governments, too.
5. Good citizens know how to get along with each other.

Tell a Story Make up a story about a trip to our country's capital or your state's capital. Tell what you saw and who you met there.

I pledge Allegiance to the flag of the United States of America And to the Republic for which it stands, One Nation under God, Indivisible, with Liberty and Justice for all.

Review

Use Vocabulary

Use the word in the box when you answer the question.

1. Is a **mayor** a leader of a city, state, or country?

2. Where does a **judge** work?

3. How many times can each person **vote** in an election?

4. How many branches does our country's **government** have?

5. What is a **freedom** Americans have?

Check Understanding

1. How do Americans honor their country?
2. What is the Constitution?
3. How does our government help us?
4. Who decides whether laws are fair?
5. How do people help their government?

Think Critically

1. Why do you think the bald eagle is a good symbol for our country?
2. Who are some people who help govern your community?
3. What are some things that good citizens do?

Apply Skills

A. How to Find Directions on a Map

Four States

1. Name two states that share a boundary.
2. What is the capital of Tennessee?
3. In what direction would you travel to go from Richmond to Frankfort?

B. How to Understand What People Think

1. Name something you have strong feelings about.
2. Give one fact and one opinion about the thing you named.

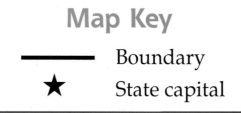

Map Key

—— Boundary

★ State capital

Read More About It

<u>In 1776</u> by Jean Marzollo. Scholastic. This book tells how our country and some of our American customs got started.

<u>Billy the Great</u> by Rosa Guy. Delacorte. Two families find a way to work out their problems and become good neighbors.

UNIT 6

Our Neighbors Near and Far

VOCABULARY

ancestor

custom

artifact

172

independence

communication

173

SET the SCENE with Literature

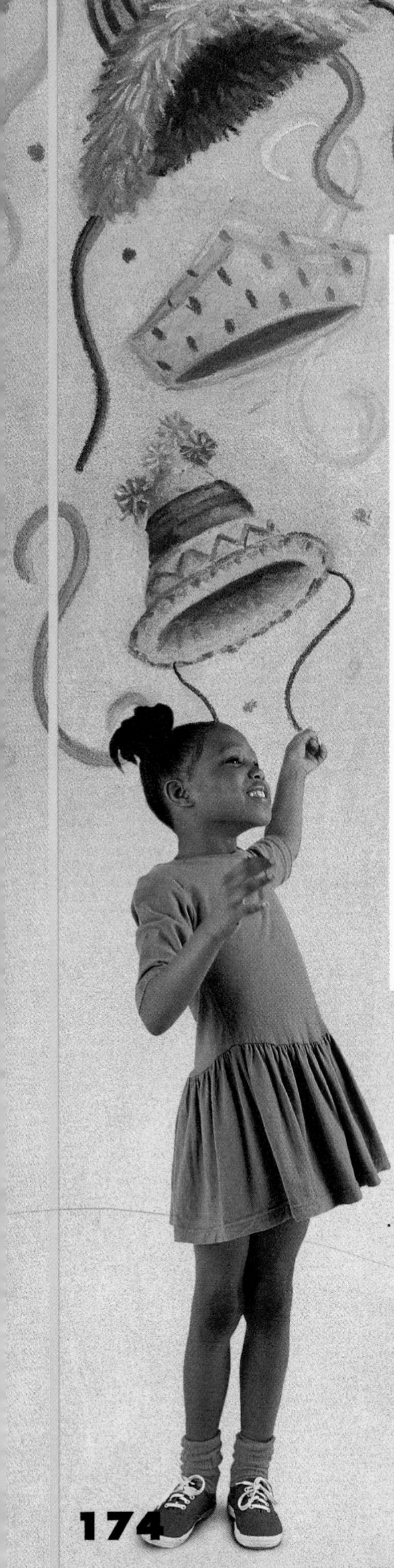

Pride

by Alma Flor Ada

Proud of my family
proud of my language
proud of my culture
proud of my race
proud to be who I am.

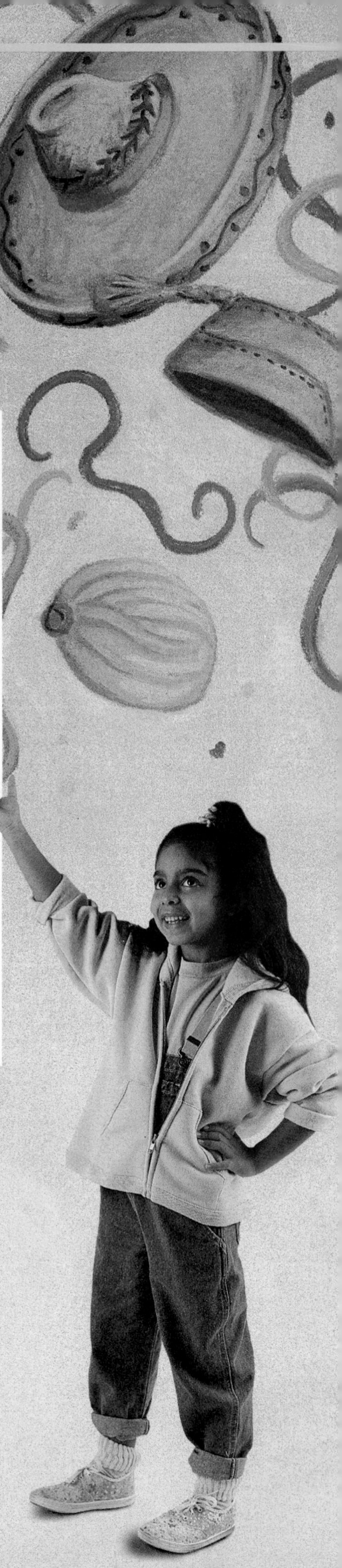

175

A World of People

Many people come from other countries to live in the United States. Join these children as they meet a new friend. See what they learn about him and about one another.

———————

Today we have a special visitor in our classroom. His name is Antonio. He is from Italy. Antonio has brought pictures of his family and his school. He likes to read books, just as we do. His books are written in the Italian language. Antonio is learning to speak English. Antonio would like to play his violin for us. He says music is a language we can all understand.

Antonio is Tina's cousin. Tina's ancestors came from Italy. **Ancestors** are people in our family who lived before us. The ancestors of many Americans came from other countries. Some of them moved here hundreds of years ago. Others have been here only a short time.

Chad's ancestors came here from Africa long ago. Emily's family moved to America from Poland when she was a baby. Cam Linh and her family just moved here from Vietnam.

Our class is making a quilt. Each of us has made one patch to tell about our families. Mine shows Grandma, me, and my bicycle. Grandma is from Ireland, so I drew a shamrock on my patch. Bobby is from Canada. He drew a maple leaf on his patch, just like the one on the Canadian flag. Carla's patch has ballet shoes and a Hopi Indian design. Her ancestors were some of the first Americans.

Our teacher says the United States is like a big quilt. Each patch is different, but together the pieces are strong and beautiful.

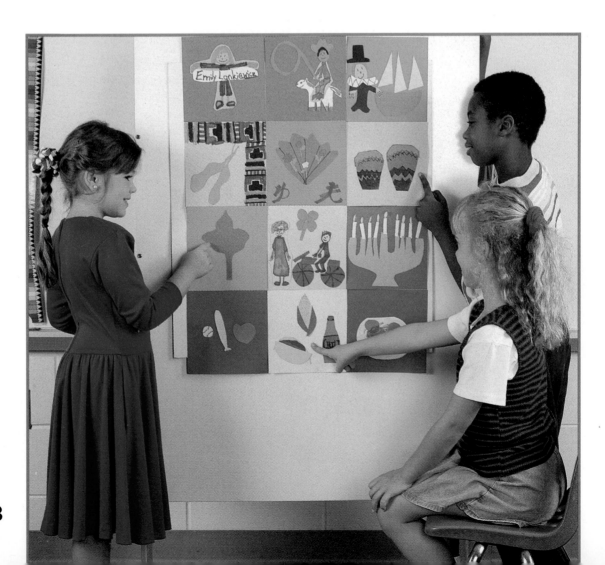

Our quilt helps us know more about one another. That makes it easier to be friends.

Why is it important to learn about other people?

SKILLS

HOW TO

Use a Bar Graph

Our class quilt tells about our ancestors. We also made a bar graph to show what parts of the world they came from. A **bar graph** is a kind of drawing that shows numbers of things.

1. Look at the bar graph. How did the children list their ancestors?

2. Find Africa on the graph. What color is the bar? What number does the bar reach? How many children have ancestors from Africa?

3. Four children have ancestors from the same continent. Which continent is that?

4. Compare the bars. From which continent do the most ancestors come? From which continent do the fewest come?

Our Ancestors

	0	1	2	3	4	5	6	7
Africa								
Asia								
North America								
South America								
Europe								
Australia								
Not Sure								

Think and Do

Work with classmates to make a bar graph. List foods from different countries. Then use the bars to show the number of children who like each food.

Community Celebrations

Chinese New Year

In some communities, families celebrate special holidays. They may wear colorful costumes and eat tasty foods. They may dance and sing songs passed down from their ancestors. Our class made a scrapbook of some of these special times.

For several days during Chinese New Year, everyone wishes each other "Gung Hay Fat Choy" or "Happy New Year." You can see bright-red decorations everywhere. People eat spring rolls and duck with rice stuffing. These are old Chinese customs. A **custom** is the way people usually do things. Another favorite custom is carrying paper lanterns through the streets behind a dancing dragon.

182

Cinco de mayo

On May 5, Mexican Americans watch parades with riders on beautiful horses. The smell of tortillas, burritos, and tamales fills the air. This is Cinco de mayo. It is a fiesta, or feast, that reminds us of the freedom Mexicans fought for long ago.

Everyone loves dancing and singing to the music of the guitars and horns. Children have fun trying to break open piñatas. The piñatas are stuffed with fruits, candies, and toys.

At the end of December, many African American families celebrate Kwanzaa. On each of the seven days, a candle is lit. The first day is Umoja, which means unity.

Kwanzaa

Kuumba is the sixth day. People wear colorful African clothing, tell old stories, and dance to African drums.

The last day is the Karamu, or feast. Black-eyed peas, ham, apple salad, corn bread, sweet-potato pie, and other delicious dishes are served.

Some African Americans celebrate another holiday called Juneteenth. On June 19 they remember how in 1865 thousands of slaves in Texas were given their freedom. Families gather at parades and picnics to tell stories about their history.

Juneteenth

On this day for giving thanks, many people join in singing the hymn, "Lift Ev'ry Voice."

"Lift ev'ry voice and sing
Till earth and heaven ring,
Ring with the harmonies of Liberty"

Greek
Epiphany

For almost 100 years Greeks in Tarpon Springs, Florida, have celebrated the Feast of the Epiphany. January 6 is an important religious holiday for them. Families parade from the church to Spring Bayou for the blessing of the water. A cross is thrown into the water, and young men dive after it. The one who finds it wins honor.

A glendi, or festival, follows with dancing and music and plenty of seafood to eat. Thousands of visitors come to Tarpon Springs every year to celebrate this exciting Greek Festival.

How does your family
or community celebrate
special times?

SKILLS
HOW TO
Learn from Artifacts

Celebrations are an important part of Native American life. The objects in the photos were made to be used in special celebrations. Objects made by people are called artifacts. Artifacts help us learn about the lives of the people who make them.

1. Look at the artifacts and read about them. Describe each artifact. How do you think each one is used?

2. What materials do the Indians use to make the objects?

3. What can you tell about the Hopis by looking at the kachina doll?

4. What can you tell about the Plains Indians from their artifact?

Hopi people use kachina dolls carved from wood to honor their ancestors.

Plains Indians use rattles made from gourds to celebrate good harvests.

Navajos believe sand paintings help in healing ceremonies.

Some Indians of the Northwest Coast honor their ancestors with carved wooden totem poles.

Corn husk masks are used by Iroquois people in special celebrations.

Think and Do

Draw a picture of an artifact that might tell someone about you.

One for All, and All for One

People around the world have the same needs. They share the same feelings about what makes life good. People everywhere think about how to keep safe and healthy and how to get along with others.

Some children in other countries made posters to show how to keep our world a good place to live. How are their ideas like yours?

Use the earth as you need it.

Henrik Kaurin
Age 8
Sweden

188

Mirna Hamady
Age 8
Abu Dhabi,
United Arab
Emirates

PEACE IS Good BECAUSE HOMES
don't get destroyed.

We have to keep the water clean.

Daniel Vargas
Age 7
Costa Rica

189

Kevyn Loggins
Age 7
Germany,
United States

Peace is at my friend's house. She lets me hold her ♥ rabbit and I say thank you very much. friendship makes peace.

Natalie Madi
Age 6 ¹/₂
Lebanon,
Czech Republic

Peace begins with me by playing nicely in the game.

Reuse or recycle.

The children made these posters to communicate their feelings. **Communication** is the sharing of ideas. When people get to know one another, they can work together to solve problems.

John Oh
Age 7
South Korea

✓ What are some ways people communicate with each other?

HOW TO

Act on Your Own

Many children are interested in helping their communities. When Kristina Swartwout was nine years old, she noticed a problem in her town of Ashland, Oregon. Cars were not stopping for children at crosswalks. Kristina wrote a letter to the Ashland, Oregon, newspaper. The mayor of Ashland read the letter and made Kristina a member of the Traffic Safety Commission.

Acting on your own is showing independence. Kristina's independent act helped make her community safer for everyone.

Kristina followed these steps:

1. Name the problem. ⟶ Children cannot cross safely.

2. Decide what you want to do. ⟶ Let people know about the problem.

3. Think of ways to act on your own to solve the problem. ⟶ Write a letter to the editor or make posters.

4. Think about what might happen. ⟶ Many people might read the letter. Fewer people might see the posters.

5. Choose the best way to solve the problem. ⟶ Write a letter to the editor.

Think and Do

Think of a problem and write a plan for solving it.

Samantha Smith: Young Peacemaker

Sometimes writing a letter can get amazing results. That is what ten-year-old Samantha Smith found out in 1982. Samantha was worried about the United States and the Soviet Union getting into a war. She decided to do something about it.

Samantha wrote to Yuri Andropov, the leader of the Soviet Union. Samantha asked Mr. Andropov how he felt about war.

To Samantha's surprise, Mr. Andropov answered her letter. He told Samantha that people in his country wanted peace just like people in the United

States. Mr. Andropov invited Samantha to visit his country.

That summer Samantha did go to the Soviet Union. Everywhere she went, people welcomed her. She made new friends at a summer camp for children.

The old Soviet Union is gone. Yet in Russia today, people still remember Samantha and the friendships she started. A statue in her hometown in Maine reminds everyone of what one person can do to bring people together around the world.

What Can You Do?

- Write to your senator or representative or to a world leader about one of your concerns.
- Make a friend in another country. Become a pen pal.

Story Cloth

Look at the pictures. They will help you remember what you learned.

Talk About the Main Ideas

1. People from many different countries live in the United States.
2. People and communities celebrate special customs.
3. People everywhere care about peace, cooperation, and a healthy world.

Make Puppets   Make a stick puppet of someone from another country. Work with a partner and use your puppets to tell why people should get along.

Review

Use Vocabulary

Give another example to help explain each word.

Word	Examples	
1. custom	Fourth of July parade	
2. independence	making your lunch	
3. artifact	an old cooking pot	
4. ancestor	great-grandmother	
5. communication	writing a letter	

Check Understanding

1. The ancestors of American citizens came from many different countries. Name three of these countries.

2. What can we learn about people from their holidays?

3. Why do people everywhere need to communicate?

4. What is one way you can make a difference in your community?

Think Critically

1. How is America like a big quilt? How does that make America strong?

2. Why do countries need to work together to protect our planet?

A. How to Use a Bar Graph

The bar graph shows some places children would like to visit.

Vacations We Would Like							
African Animal Park							
European Castles							
South American Rain Forest							
Australian Kangaroo Ranch							
0	1	2	3	4	5	6	7

1. What choices did the children have?
2. Which place was chosen by the most children?
3. Which place was chosen by the fewest children?

B. How to Learn from Artifacts

What might you learn from looking at this arrowhead?

Read More About It

Family Pictures by Carmen Lomas Garza. Children's Book Press. An artist paints and writes about family customs.

The Wonderful Towers of Watts by Patricia Zelver. Tambourine. This is the story of how one man helped make his neighborhood beautiful.

GLOSSARY

A

ancestor

Someone in a family who lived long ago. My **ancestor** came to America from England. (page 177)

artifact

Something that is made and used by people. This bowl is an Indian **artifact**. (page 186)

B

bar graph

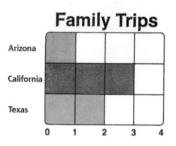

Family Trips

	0	1	2	3	4
Arizona					
California					
Texas					

A picture that shows how many or how much. This **bar graph** shows the states one family has visited. (page 180)

boundary

Indiana Ohio

A line that shows where one state ends and another begins. The red line shows the **boundary** between Indiana and Ohio. (page 152)

C

Maryland
Washington, D. C.
Virginia

capital

A city in which government leaders meet and work. Washington, D.C., is the **capital** of the United States. (page 90)

citizen

A member of a community. Pedro is a **citizen** of the United States. (page 22)

city

A large community where people live and work. New York City is the largest **city** in the United States. (page 14)

communication

Sharing ideas with others. Many people use telephones for **communication**. (page 191)

community

A place where people live and the people who live there. The **community** I live in is a big city. (page 11)

compass rose

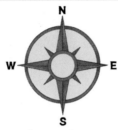

Arrows on a map that show directions. The **compass rose** shows which way is north, south, east, and west. (page 152)

Congress

Our country's lawmakers. The **Congress** of the United States meets in the Capitol Building. (page 91)

conservation

Working to save resources or make them last longer. Forest rangers teach us about the **conservation** of trees. (page 64)

consumer

A person who buys and uses goods and services. This **consumer** is buying food for a picnic. (page 125)

continent

One of the largest bodies of land on the Earth. We live on the **continent** of North America. (page 44)

country

A land and the people who live in that land. The United States is one of three **countries** in North America. (page 22)

crop

A kind of plant that people grow for food or other uses. Corn is an important **crop** in the United States. (page 47)

custom

A way of doing something. Eating with chopsticks is a **custom** in many Asian countries. (page 182)

D

desert

A dry place. Very little rain falls in a **desert**. (page 35)

diagram

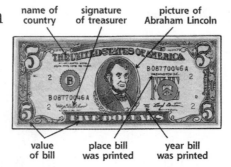

A drawing that shows the parts of something. The **diagram** shows the parts of a five-dollar bill. (page 130)

direction

North, south, east, or west. The sign tells us in which **direction** to go. (page 152)

E

election

The time when people vote. The **election** for President is in November. (page 146)

equator

A line on a map or globe that is halfway between the North Pole and the South Pole. The weather at the **equator** is hot. (page 45)

F

factory

A place where things are made. This **factory** makes shoes. (page 114)

freedom

The right of people to make their own choices. Americans have the **freedom** to worship as they please. (page 155)

G

geography

The study of the Earth and its people. Some maps show the **geography** of a place. (page 32)

globe

A model of the Earth. We have a big **globe** in our classroom. (page 44)

goods

Things that people make or grow. People who play soccer buy these **goods**. (page 16)

government

A group of people who make the laws for a community or a country. There are people from each state in the United States **government**. (page 148)

grid

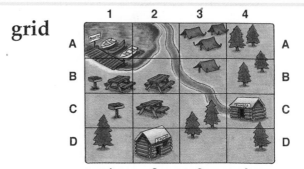

Lines that cross one another to form boxes. The lines of a **grid** can help you find places on a map. (page 94)

group

A number of people doing something together. This **group** is making music. (page 4)

H

history

The story of what has happened in a place. This picture book is about the **history** of our country. (page 78)

holiday

A time to celebrate. The Fourth of July is an American **holiday**. (page 142)

I

income

The money people earn for the work they do. I am saving part of my **income** to buy a computer. (page 126)

independence

The freedom of people to choose their own government and make their own laws. On the Fourth of July, we celebrate our country's **independence**. (page 192)

invention

Something that has been made for the first time. The first lightbulb was an important **invention**. (page 96)

island

Hawaii

Land that has water all around it. The state of Hawaii is made up of many **islands**. (page 36)

J

judge

Someone who works as a leader in court. The **judge** ruled that Mrs. Page had broken the law. (page 150)

L

lake

A body of water that has land all around it. People from all around the **lake** use it for fishing. (page 37)

landform

A kind of land. Mountains, hills, and plains are **landforms**. (page 34)

landmark

A familiar object at a place. The Alamo is a Texas **landmark**. (page 84)

law

A rule that everyone must follow. The **law** says cars must stop at a stop sign. (page 15)

lawmaker

A leader who makes laws. Many **lawmakers** work in our state capital. (page 91)

leader

The person who helps a group plan what to do. A principal is the **leader** of a school. (page 6)

M

map

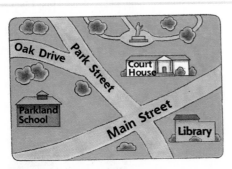

A drawing that shows where places are. We can find the library on the **map**. (page 13)

map key

A list of the symbols on a map. The **map key** tells what the symbols on a map stand for. (page 18)

mayor

One of a city's most important leaders. The **mayor** meets with the lawmakers of our community. (page 155)

monument

Something set up to honor someone or something. This **monument** honors George Washington. (page 92)

motto

A word or short saying that tells a feeling or an idea. Our country's **motto** is "In God We Trust." (page 142)

mountain

The highest kind of land. There is snow on these **mountains**. (page 34)

N

needs

Things people cannot live without. Food, clothing, and a place to live are **needs**. (page 9)

neighborhood

A small part of a community. Our **neighborhood** has a fruit-and-vegetable market. (page 8)

O

ocean

A very large body of salty water. The Pacific **Ocean** is west of the United States, and the Atlantic **Ocean** is east of it. (page 36)

P

pictograph

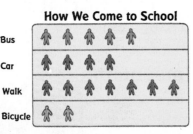

How We Come to School

Bus	🚶🚶🚶🚶🚶
Car	🚶🚶🚶🚶
Walk	🚶🚶🚶🚶🚶🚶
Bicycle	🚶🚶

A picture that uses symbols to show numbers of things. This **pictograph** shows how the children in one class come to school. (page 112)

plain

Land that is mostly flat. Our farm is on a **plain**. (page 35)

prediction

Something a person says will happen. Tom's **prediction** is that it is going to rain. (page 119)

President

The leader of the United States. George Washington was our country's first **President**. (page 90)

producer

A person who makes or grows something. Factory and farm workers are **producers**. (page 124)

R

resource

Something people use that comes from the Earth. Wood is an important **resource**. (page 51)

river

A long body of water that flows through the land. The Mississippi River is the longest **river** in the United States. (page 37)

route

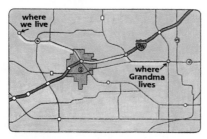

A way to go from one place to another. The map shows the **route** to Grandma's house. (page 94)

rule

Something you must or must not do. A good **rule** for home and school is "Put things away after using them." (page 6)

S

services

Jobs people do that help others. Firefighters, police officers, and teachers provide **services**. (page 17)

settler

A person who makes a home in a new place. **Settlers** from many countries built homes in the West. (page 78)

state

TEXAS

A part of our country. The United States has fifty **states**. (page 152)

suburb

A community near a city. We live in a **suburb** of Chicago. (page 33)

symbol

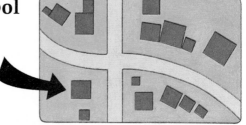

A picture that stands for something real. A square is a **symbol** for a store on this map. (page 18)

T

table

| My Best Friends | |
Boys	Girls
Nick	Tonya
Peter	Meg
Don	

Lists of things in groups. This **table** shows my best friends. (page 62)

taxes

Money people pay to their government. This man's **taxes** will pay for community services. (page 110)

time line

A line that shows when things happened. This **time line** shows when Fred took trips this year. (page 82)

trade

Give money, goods, or services to get something in return. Mari wants to **trade** her book to Nancy for a game. (page 120)

transportation

Any way of moving people or things from place to place. Airplanes are one kind of **transportation**. (page 120)

V

valley

Low land between hills or mountains. A small river runs through the **valley**. (page 34)

vote

A choice that gets counted. The person who gets the most **votes** is the winner. (page 146)

W

wants

Things people would like to have. A new car is one of my family's **wants**. (page 126)

INDEX

Photo Credits:
Key: (t) top; (b) bottom; (l) left; (r) right; (c) center

Table of Contents
Harcourt Brace and Company: iii Rich Franco; vi Terry Sinclair; vii Rich Franco; viii Rich Franco.
Other: iv John Elk/Tony Stone Images; v R. Moore/Superstock.

Unit 1
Harcourt Brace and Company: A8 (bc) Julie Fletcher; 1 (bl) Terry Sinclair; 2, 3 (inset), 4, 5 (t) Rich Franco; 5 (c) Terry Sinclair; 5 (b), 6 (b), 7 (t), (b) Rich Franco; 8, 9, 10 (tl), (bl), (br), (inset) 11 (br), (inset) Terry Sinclair; 14 (c), 15 (c), 16 (c), 17 (c) Victoria Bowen; 14 (tl), 15 (inset), 16 (bl), 17 (tr), (b), Richard Haynes; 22 (b), 23 (t) Victoria Bowen; 23 (bl) Terry Sinclair.

Other: A8, 1 (t) Kindra Clineff/Picture Cube, The; A8 (bl) Bob Daemmrich/Stock, Boston; A8 (br) Telegraph Colour Library/FPG International; 1 (bc) Gabe Palmer/Stock Market, The; 1 (br) John Scheiber/Stock Market, The; 10 (cl) Richard Slocaton/Stockhouse, Inc., The; 11 (tl) Don Smetzer/Tony Stone Images; 11 (tr) David Young-Wolff/PhotoEdit; 11 (cr) G. Schaub/Superstock; 12 (c) Alex S. MacLean; 14 (bl) E. F. Productions/Superstock; 14 (br) Gala/Superstock; 15 (tl) C. Orrico/Superstock; 15 (tr) David M. Barron/Oxygen Group Photography; 15 (br) Glod Collection/Superstock; 16 (tl) Owen Franken/Stock, Boston; 22 (tl) Andy Sacks/Tony Stone Images; 22 (c) Lawrence Migdale/Stock, Boston; 23 (tl) C. Frank Crzus/FPG; 23 (tcl) Steven Peters/Tony Stone Images; 23 (tcr) Paul Conklin/PhotoEdit; 23 (tr) Prettyman M/R/PhotoEdit; 23 (cl) Robert Brenner/PhotoEdit; 23 (c) Dennis MacDonald/PhotoEdit; 23 (cr) Bob Daemmrich Photography, Inc.; 23 (br) Wayne Hoy/Picture Cube, The.

Unit 2
Harcourt Brace and Company: 29 (bl); 31 (br) Rich Franco; 44 (c); 49 (b) Jerry White; 64 (tr).
Other: 28, 29 (t) Mark Segal/Tony Stone Images; 28 (bc) Pete Saloutos/Stock Market, The; 28 (br) Sterling FX/The Image Bank; 29 (bc) Rich Iwasaki/Tony Stone Images; 32 (bl) Peter Cortez/Tony Stone Images; 32 (cr) John Elk/Tony Stone Images; 33 (t) David R. Frazier; 33 (b) Richard Pasley/Stock, Boston; 34 (t) Ed Cooper Photo; 35 (t) Craig Aurness/Westlight; 35 (b) J. Randklev/Allstock; 36 (t) George Hunter/Tony Stone Images; 36 (b) Simeone Huber/Tony Stone Images; 37 (t) Grant Heilman/Grant Heilman Photography; 37 (b) Holt Confer/Grant Heilman; 40 (tl) Keith Wood/Tony Stone Images; 40 (cl) Art Wolfe/Allstock; 40 (bl) Fredrick McKinney/FPG; 40 (br) Tony Stone Images/Raymond Barnes; 41 (tr) Suzanne Murphy-Larronde/FPG International; 41 (cr) Tony Stone Images/Doug Armand; 41 (br) Tony Stone Images/Richard Bradbury; 41 (bl) Farrell Grehan/FPG International; 42 (bg) Jan Butchofsky-Houser; 42 (tl) Lawrence Migdale/PIX; 42 (tr) Chris Corrie/Sante Fe Convention and Visitors Bureau; 42 (c) Buddy Mays/International Stock; 42 (b) Lawrence Migdale/PIX; 43 (tr) Lawrence Migdale/PIX; 43 (bl) Lawrence Migdale/PIX; 46, 47 (bg) E. Streichan/Superstock; 46 (cl) FPG International; 46 (cr) FPG International; 46 (b) FPG International; 48 (t)

Chuck Pefley/Allstock; 48 (b) Andy Sacks/Tony Stone Images; 49 (tr) Visual Horizons/FPG International; 64 (b) Lawrence Migdale/PIX; 65 (tr) Lawrence Migdale/PIX; 65 (cr) Phil Degginger/Bruce Coleman, Inc.; 65 (bl) Lawrence Migdale/PIX; 66 (tr) Tony Stone Images/Lawrence Migdale; 66 (cr) John Shaw/Bruce Coleman, Inc.; 66 (bl) Lawrence Migdale/PIX; 67 (l) Bob Firth/ International Stock; 68, 69 Courtesy of Tree Musketeers; 73 (t) John Shaw/Bruce Coleman, Inc.; 73 (tc) Murial Orans; 73 (c) Jose Carrillo/PhotoEdit; 73 (bc) Norman Tomalin/Bruce Coleman, Inc.; 73 (b) Joy Spurr/Bruce Coleman, Inc.

Unit 3
Harcourt Brace and Company: 76 (br) Terry Sinclair; 90 (bl) Terry Sinclair; 96 (b) National Park Service Edison National Historic Site.

Other: 74, 75 (t) Paul Conklin/PhotoEdit; 74 (bl) Ted Hooper/Folio; 74 (br) DC Productions/Image Bank, The; 75 (bl) Everett C. Johnson/Folio; 75 (br) Michael Freeman; 76 (bl) Picture Network International; 78 (tl) Dave G. Houser; 78 (b) Michael Philip Manheim/International Stock Photography; 79 (t) Phyllis Picardi/International Stock; 79 (cl) Phyllis Picardi/International Stock; 79 (cr) Ned Haines/Photo Researchers; 79 (br) Claudia Parks/Stock Market; 80 (t) Photri; 80 (bl) Lou Jones/Image Bank, The; 80 (br) Dave G. Houser; 81 (c) Mary Ann Hemphill/Photo Researchers; 84 (cl) Bill Stanton/International Stock Photo; 84 (b) Photri; 85 (t) James P. Rowan/Tony Stone Worldwide; 85 (br) David R. Frazier Photolibrary; 86 (t) Dave G. Houser; 86 (br) David R. Frazier Photolibrary; 87 (b) Richard Stockton/Stockhouse, The; 88 (bl) The Institute of Texan Cultures, The San Antonio Light Collection; 88 (bc) The Institute of Texan Cultures, San Antonio, Texas. Courtesy of Capt. T.K.Treadwell.; 88 (cr) Charles B. Turril Collection/The Center for American History, The University of Texas at Austin; 89 (c) Bettmann Archive, The; 90 (b) Tony Stone Images; 91 (tl) Doug Armand/Tony Stone Images; 91 (tr) T. Zavier/Washington Stock Photo Inc.; 92 (tl) M. Rossler/Superstock; 92 (tc) C.P. Gridley/FPG International; 92 (br) TPS/Superstock; 93 (c) Maxwell Mackenzie/Tony Stone Images; 93 (b) Jack Novak/Photri; 96 (t) National Portrait Gallery, Smithsonian Institute/Art Resource, NY; 97 (t) The Granger Collection, N.Y.; 97 (b) David Burnett/Contact Press Images; 98 (tl) National Portrait Gallery, Washington, DC/Art Resource, NY; 98 (br) R. Moore/Superstock; 99 (tr) New York Public Library; 100 (tl) Bob Burch/Stockhouse, The; 100 (tc) Ed Bock/Stockhouse, The; 100 (tr) A. Guidry; 101 (tl) H. Abernathy/H. Armstrong Roberts, Inc.; 101 (tc) Two of Diamonds/Stockhouse, The; 101 (tr) Jim Armstrong/Omni-Photo Communications.

Unit 4
Harcourt Brace and Company: 106, 107 (t) Terry Sinclair; 106 (bl) Rich Franco; 107 (br) Rich Franco; 109 (inset) Rich Franco; 110 (bl) Terry D. Sinclair; 114 (tr) Earl Kogler; 114 (b), 115 (b), 116 (b), 117 (b) Victoria Bowen; 117 (bg) Terry Sinclair; 119 (t) Rich Franco; 120 (bg), 121 (bg), 122 (bg), 123 (bg) Victoria Bowen; 121 (tr), 121 (c inset), 122 (bl), 124 (b), 125 (t) Terry Sinclair; 126 (c), 127 (bl) Rich Franco; 128 (tl) Earl Kogler; 128 (tr) Rob Downey; 128 (bl) Rich Franco; 128 (br) Eric Camden; 129 (tl), (b) Rich Franco; 133 (br) Victoria Bowen.

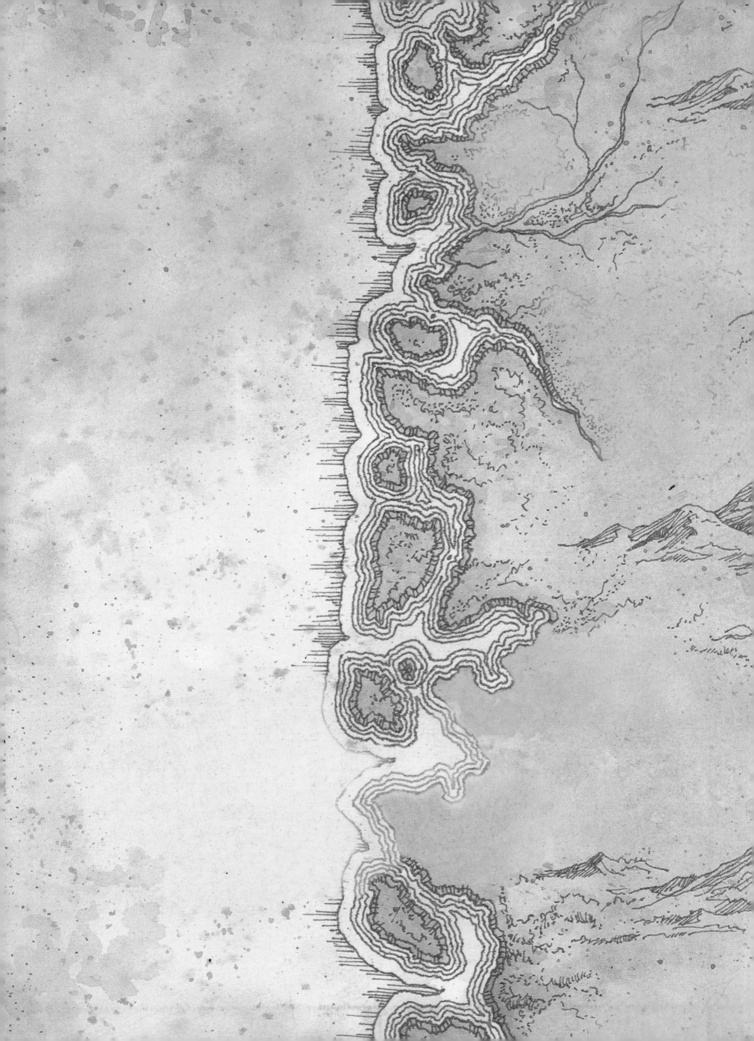